Ubon

The Last Camp Before Freedom

*The untold story of a Japanese POW camp
in north-east Thailand*

Ray Withnall

ISBN: 9798642415597

PublishNation
www.publishnation.co.uk

For Mum and Dad

CONTENTS

ACKNOWLEDGEMENTS

I am indebted to several people for the help they provided in writing about Thailand and Ubon's Japanese Prisoner of War camp during World War Two.

In particular to Khun Orathai, the secretary of a group of retired Ubon professionals who voluntarily promote and support their community. Her enthusiasm led her to find invaluable sources of local information and individuals who recalled their memories of the Japanese and the Prisoners in Ubon. Without her exuberance much of Ubon's World War Two history would be lost.

I would like to thank the rest of the group for their kindness and the welcome they extend to me each time I visit Ubon. Especially to Khun Kasem Boonrom for his encouragement and friendship.

My thanks also go to those individuals in Ubon who willingly spent time talking about their memories of World War Two. Amongst them were Khun Orain Phuriphat, a former member of parliament and whose father, Nai Thongin Phuriphat, was the leader of the Seri Thai in Ubon and a member of the Thai Government. Khun Suwit Koonphul, Khun Gim Jiarajinda, Khun U-phai, Khun Hein Nam Lee, Liang Kaiw and Khun Ratanapon Sihpanom.

But special thanks and appreciation goes to Khun Thongdee Wongman. He has lived in Ban Nong Phai, the village in which the Ubon camp was located, for all of his eighty-seven years and vividly remembers the Prisoners and their captors. Without his help much of this story would have been missed.

I have also had the privilege and honour of meeting Tom Brown, Harold Pleasance and Maurice Naylor who were sent to Ubon to construct the airstrip. Just to meet them was special but by talking to them about their memories of Ubon I felt I was touching history.

I have met many relatives of ex-Ubon prisoners who have willingly shared copies of letters, photographs, drawings and sketches. In particular I acknowledge my gratitude to Kathy Knott, Timothy Whitehead, Fenella French, David Sartin, Julie Summers, Liz Rowbotham, Xan Smiley, Philip Smiley, Anthony Wilder and Mike Clarke.

Amongst the FEPOW community there are many people who willingly share information and their help is very much appreciated. I thank them all.

Finally, my thanks go to my wife, Khamma, who has whole heartedly supported my passion for this story about her hometown. She has patiently attended many meetings with me to translate proceedings and conversations into English. She has been a fantastic help when surveying and investigating the site of the camp and airstrip and on many other occasions at places where my inquisitive nature has taken us.

PREFACE

My late father, Joseph Withnall, was a proud soldier of the 51st Highland Division, Black Watch and a survivor of the Normandy landings in June 1944. He fought through Europe to Bremerhaven in Germany where in May 1945 he marched in the victory parade. He received the Legion d'Honneur for his contribution in the liberation of France.

When I was a young boy, he inspired me with bedtime stories of his courage and bravery. After he retired he became a member of the Stockport Normandy Veterans Association. I cherish the memories of the pilgrimages to Normandy I made with my parents and the NVA. Through such visits I began to realise the enormity of the sacrifices made by all servicemen in World War Two.

I had the foresight to ask my father about his childhood days and his experience and feelings as a nineteen-year-old soldier facing the enormity of war. His war-time encounters add significant and unique detail to events only generally described in many World War Two books.

Energised by piecing together my father's story, I was aware that my knowledge of World War Two was in dire need of improvement. This was especially so of Thailand, where I was spending much of time.

Khamma, my wife, lives in Ubon Ratchathani in north-east Thailand. In January 2015 we embarked on a road trip to follow the infamous Thai–Burma railway. We travelled through Kanchanaburi to the Three Pagodas Pass, which is on the border with Burma, stopping at many of the locations along the Death Railway.

At Kanchanaburi we visited the Commonwealth War Graves Commission cemetery to pay our respects to the Prisoners of War who perished whilst building the railway. Amongst its many graves we came across Sergeant Arthur Horace Withnell, an Australian from the 2/3 Machine Gun Battalion. The similarity to my surname struck a chord.

Standing by his beautifully tended grave I decided to educate myself about the Thai–Burma railway, and the Prisoners of War who had worked on it, through the eyes of Sergeant Arthur. I wanted to know his story and we started by visiting the iconic Thai–Burma Railway Centre where I obtained Sergeant Arthur's military details.

I discovered that he had died from cholera at Hell Fire Pass. With the help of the internet I traced him to his hometown of Northam in Western Australia and followed his war-time career to the Middle East then to Java, where he was captured by the Japanese. I even made contact with his family, who willingly sent me more details. They told me Arthur had a brother who was a POW with him on the railway and survived the war.

Then one day, I was at our home in Ubon casually reading the Facebook page of the excellent *Researching FEPOW History Group*. My attention was drawn to a comment referring to a POW camp in a place called Ubon. I was instantly intrigued. So began my quest to discover the history of the camp. The only tangible evidence available to me at that time was a memorial called the Monument of Merit, allegedly constructed by the Prisoners located in Ubon's central park at Thung Si Muang.

I discovered the end of the story before I knew its beginning. The Ubon camp was only open for the six months preceding the end of the War in Asia in August 1945. It was a prison camp from which 3,000 men re-gained their freedom after 3½ years of brutal incarceration. Most of them had worked on the infamous Thai-Burma railway and all of them had suffered unimaginable deprivation and brutality.

I learnt that Ubon camp's liberation involved the British Special Operations Executive and the Seri Thai resistance movement. Their participation revealed a mélange of national and international politics mixed with military ambition to defeat the Japanese. This led my curiosity to inquire how a peace-loving Thailand became entangled with the merciless Japanese. There appeared to be more events related to the story of Ubon than I imagined. This is where the Ubon story begins.

My attention was also drawn to the certainty that the story of the Ubon camp did not end when the Japanese surrendered or even when last ex-Prisoner went home. The SOE had to dis-arm 9,000 Japanese soldiers and hold them before their eventual repatriation to Japan. They also had to resolve nationalistic unrest across the border in French Indochina, which on one occasion ended in tragedy. Ubon was not restored to normality overnight.

Whilst talking to local elders the true story of the legendary 'Little Mother of Ubon' emerged. They talked about welcoming the men into their homes and providing entertainment whilst they waited for repatriation. These unselfish acts are called *merit making* in traditional Buddhist parlance, and are annually commemorated at Ubon's Service of Remembrance held at Monument of Merit.

The FEPOW Prayer

And we that are left grow old with the years
Remembering the heartache, the pain and the tears.
Hoping and praying that never again
Man will sink to such sorrow and shame.
The price that was paid we will always remember
Every day, every month, not just in November

INTRODUCTION

There are many accounts, books and movies retelling the atrocious plight of Allied Prisoners of War held by the Japanese during World War Two. They graphically depict the deprivation, cruelty and humiliation inflicted upon thousands of Allied military personnel and innocent civilians by the Japanese between 1942 and 1945. In particular there are harrowing accounts of Prisoners and Romusha (South East Asian civilians) sent to Thailand and Burma to build a railway in seemingly impossible conditions. These horrendous stories tell of the death and survival of Prisoners forced to work for the Japanese in a country which was hitherto associated with peace, friendship and people with a charming smile. How did Thailand, so proud of its neutrality and independence, become associated with Japan? What was the feeling amongst the Thai people towards the Japanese and the Prisoners of War? How did the war end for Thailand? The answers to these questions can be found in the story of the Japanese Prisoner of War camp at a small town in the north-east of Thailand called Ubon.

The Ubon Prisoner of War camp only existed for the last six months of the war. This makes it a significant camp for the 3,000 men incarcerated there simply because it was the camp from which they were liberated. The end of hostilities in August 1945 and the subsequent liberation create a special story for all occupied camps, and Ubon is no exception. The events leading up to the liberation of the Ubon camp were led by British Special Operations Executive (SOE) officer Major David Smiley, working alongside the Seri Thai, Thailand's resistance movement. After the liberation, the generosity and compassion from the people of Ubon helped the men considerably to re-adjust to their freedom.

In December 1941, the Thai government allowed the Japanese a *'right of free passage'* over Thai territory. Within weeks of this

13

decision, the Thai government declared war on Great Britain, the United States and its Allies. After these belligerent acts it might be expected that ordinary Thai people would not show any sympathy to enemy Prisoners of War imprisoned in their country. This was not the case. Many Thai people showed courage, generosity and compassion and some were prepared to risk their lives to help the Prisoners in whatever way they could. Eventually Thailand's distrust and dislike of Japanese high handedness was channelled into an organised resistance movement called the Seri Thai. The leaders of the Seri Thai had to convince the Allies to support them against the Japanese. This was no easy task but, as the Japanese stronghold began to weaken, the Allies came forward with military supplies, arms and training.

In 1933, after Thailand abstained from voting in a League of Nations motion to expel Japan following its invasion of Manchuria, Japan began to encourage political, cultural and military alliances and relations, which Thailand found difficult to refuse. It was also the period in which Japan was espousing a strategy for a *'Greater East Asia Co-Prosperity Sphere'*, which aimed to create a bloc of Asian nations led by Japan and free from Western influence.

In 1932 a peaceful coup d'état in Thailand brought an end to an absolute monarchy and introduced a constitutional monarchy led by ambitious politicians. Among them were Luang Pridi Banomyong and Field Marshall Luang Phibul Songkhram. Both were ambitious young men but, as the decade progressed, they developed differing and opposing views. Luang Pridi opposed the Japanese presence but in 1941, in his position as prime minister, Luang Phibul decided that the Japanese could use Thailand to attack the British held Malaya, Singapore and Burma.

The new government introduced social change but failed to entice and excite the poor rural subsistence agricultural regions such as Ubon, situated 350 miles north east of Bangkok in the relatively remote region of north-east Thailand. Ubon already had an airfield and a rail link to Bangkok but, even so, high-level politics did not capture the imagination of the Ubon community. However, its proximity to the disputed border with Laos and Cambodia (known then as French Indochina) led to the establishment of an army garrison with air cover to monitor the border area.

Almost immediately after the Japanese entered Thailand in December 1941, Luang Pridi formed a guerrilla organisation, which became known as the Seri Thai Movement. Its main objective was to gain the support of Great Britain and the United States to help drive the Japanese out of Thailand. However, the task was made extremely difficult when Prime Minister Luang Phibul declared war on the Allies in January 1942, making it unlikely they would support the Seri Thai cause.

Three years later, towards the end of 1944, the situation had changed. Luang Phibul was replaced by a new government that refused to bow to further Japanese demands for more finance to support their operations in Thailand. This act of defiance allowed Luang Pridi to convince the Allies that the majority popular opinion in Thailand was anti-Japanese and, with their support, the Seri Thai could raise a credible fighting force. After losing the battles of Imphal and Kohima, the Japanese faced an increasing threat of defeat, which offered the Allies an opportunity. After agreements at diplomatic levels the Allies, through their respective 'special military services', supplied the Seri Thai with arms, sabotage training and intelligence gathering.

The impact of World War Two did not arrive in Ubon until February 1945 when Allied Prisoners of War began to arrive to build an airstrip for the Japanese. The remoteness of Ubon gave the men a feeling of isolation, but in May the British SOE Force 136 sent Major David de Crespigny Smiley to the area to train and arm hundreds of Seri Thai guerrillas and at least the Prisoners' presence was discovered.

Major Smiley began to organise the Seri Thai but this suddenly changed when, in August 1945, the Japanese surrendered following the Hiroshima and Nagasaki atom bombs. Major Smiley's responsibilities changed overnight; his task now was to ensure the safety and repatriation of the men, arrange the Japanese surrender and disarm an estimated 9,000 Japanese military personnel. However he was frustrated by orders to remain undercover until he received a special code word.

The story does not end there. There was the immediate aftermath of resistance from nationalist groups in French Indochina who threatened innocent lives and resisted the return of a regime of colonial control. The safety of the area had to be secured so that people could return to peace.

This story is the sum of many parts. It focuses on the Ubon camp and the airstrip the men were forced to build, culminating in their liberation. But it also draws on the little-known contribution of the Seri Thai Movement and its growth at the hands of its leader, Luang Pridi. This includes the political differences within the Thai government and the struggle and determination to convince Great Britain and the United States that they were worthy allies and not belligerents. There is also an ever-present sense of pervading generosity and kindness from Thai people in general and Ubon in particular. This is remembered every year at the annual Service of Remembrance where expats and Thais come together to remember not only those who gave their lives for their country, but also the continuing importance of charity and benevolence in Ubon's society.

As a mark of respect to all Allied Prisoners of War, I have used a capital letter on the word Prisoner. Also, I have used the convention of addressing Thai people with their Thai title, e.g. Luang and Khun.

Transliteration of the Thai language into English varies and Thai words often appear with many different English spellings. I have tried to keep to one convention, especially with names of people and villages.

LEST WE FORGET

16

PART 1

THAILAND DRIFTS INTO WAR

Chapter 1

DECADE OF CHANGE

In 1932 Thailand's political landscape changed significantly after the bloodless coup d'état. The absolutist monarchy was replaced by a democratic regime and a promise of a revised constitution. The monarchy became ceremonial with a much-reduced power base and has remained in this form ever since. The new government was soon embroiled in serious domestic and international issues culminating in finding itself in the South East Asia War as a *de facto* ally of Japan. It was a turbulent period in a long, illustrious history.

Thailand's drift into war effectively began in 1933 at a meeting of the League of Nations. Thailand abstained in a vote to expel Japan for its invasion of Manchuria. Its ambassador explained that Thailand was a neutral country. Although it was not meant as a vote of support, Japan appreciated Thailand's position and took the opportunity to cultivate close diplomatic ties. They introduced generous trade agreements, exchange programmes of education, arts and culture, and provided military advice and co-operation. Japanese businessmen and industrial experts travelled to Thailand to guide and assist in development. But these intentions were far from honourable; Japan was spying and gathering intelligence to exploit Thailand to advance its strategic position in South East Asia.

On the domestic front, the government was failing. Political tensions rapidly developed inside the cabinet and civil unrest broke out on the streets of Bangkok. The government collapsed in 1938, leaving the military to seize power and appoint the overpowering Field Marshall Luang Phibul as prime minister. He further encouraged Japanese relations who supported his right-wing political agenda and sense of nationalism. Luang Phibul reportedly empathised with Adolf Hitler's style of dictatorship, and endorsed Japan's entry into the Axis treaty with Germany and Italy. Through Luang Phibul, Japan saw an opportunity to gain a stronger foothold in Thailand in their pursuit of domination of the region.

Thailand was now walking on a tightrope. For centuries the country had successfully resisted foreign domination, rule or colonisation, unlike its neighbours in Burma, Malaya, Singapore and French Indochina and even further south in the Dutch East Indies. The Thai people were fiercely proud of their record of independence, sovereignty and neutrality but Japan was about to tip the scales. The Thai government began to split and tensions ran high. The young finance minister, Luang Pridi, and foreign minister, Luang Direk Jayanama, appealed to the British and American Allies for assistance in deterring the Japanese.

On 12 June 1940, Thailand signed separate non-aggression treaties with France, Britain and Japan. The Thai government saw the treaty with France as an opportunity to resolve outstanding border issues along the Mekong, including the border close to Ubon. The French agreed to talk but, two days after signing the treaty, events in Europe changed the course of the relationship. Hitler's German army invaded France and this threw the administration of French Indochina into disarray. Hitler allowed a weakened French, under the Vichy government, to administer areas in which he had little or no strategic interest. Its scope extended to French Indochina, but was immediately ineffective.

At this time Japan was still at war with China, but the fighting was at a stalemate. The Japanese divisions in southern China recognised an opportunity to exploit the weakened French-Indochinese and extend their strategy to dominate South East Asia. They sought permission to cross into French Indochina in the northern Tonkin area. The Vichy government had no choice but to agree because Japan had just signed the Axis treaty with Germany and Italy and they automatically supported Japan's demands.

An agreement allowed 25,000 Japanese troops to enter the Tonkin area, but within days the Japanese reneged and advanced with 30,000 fully armed troops. The French army put up some resistance but could not defend their territory and were defeated within five days. Japanese forces streamed into French Indochina and gained a foothold on the strategic northern border with China. Not long after that, they demanded free passage through the country. The Vichy government was powerless and the French troops were hopelessly outnumbered and ill equipped. In subsequent months, the Japanese constructed strategic airfields, advance bases and headquarters in preparation for a further advance in South East Asia.

As a result of the change in administration, the Vichy French called off the border negotiations with the Thai government. But tension was running high and isolated skirmishes broke out, including in the area between Ubon and the French Indochina border town of Pakse, eighty miles due east. Royal Thai Army and Air Force bases in Ubon created natural targets. Newspaper reports recorded several attacks on Ubon during December 1940 and notably in early January 1941, when the French dropped forty bombs on Ubon. Troops based in Ubon also advanced west towards Siam Reap. Neither side declared a state of war but periodic clashes continued until 17 January 1941 when the French navy defeated the Thai navy at the battle at Koh Chang in the Gulf of Thailand. It was time for mediation. Great Britain and the United States did not want to get involved but this reluctance played into Japanese hands to exploit their ulterior motives.

By now, the Japanese had great influence over the Thai government and had successfully consolidated their territorial advantage in French Indochina. Thailand was crucial to the next stage of their expansionist plan. The Japanese calculated that if they mediated in a peace treaty between Thailand and France, they could easily broker an agreement favouring Thailand, which they could then use in the future to cajole the Thai government into returning the favour by allowing the Japanese the *'right of free passage'* over Thai territory in their plan to invade Malaya, Singapore and Burma.

Chapter 2

GATHERING DARK CLOUDS
OF WAR

By the summer of 1941, Japanese strategists occupied Saigon in French Indochina and were planning to invade Malaya, Singapore, and Burma. Thousands of Japanese troops were based on Hai Nan island for intensive training in jungle warfare, which was very different from the fighting in China campaign. They practised beach landings, living in monsoon conditions, managing tropical diseases and undertook endless exercises in jungle fighting and tactics. They forced Annamese civilians to build strategic airstrips, in particular at Phu Quok island off the south west coast of Vietnam, from where reconnaissance flights departed to gather intelligence and find weaknesses in key tactical areas along the Thai coastline of the Gulf of Thailand.

Emperor Hirohito approved the plans in October 1941 and preparations began to enter Thailand. The main invasion targets were Singora and Pattani on the east coast of the Gulf of Thailand. After the Japanese army landed, they planned to move south west and advance down the west side of Malaya, driving the Allied forces back towards Singapore. Another division was to land on the Malayan coast at Kota Bharu and advance south down the east side of Malaya. The two divisions planned to meet at Johor Bahru opposite Singapore Island, before attacking Singapore.

To carry out these attacks they needed the Thai government, represented by Prime Minister Luang Phibul, to grant them the *'right of free passage'* through the Kingdom of Thailand. However, in the months prior to the formal request, members of the Thai cabinet, in particular foreign minister Luang Jayanama, anticipated the Japanese plans and lobbied the British and

American legations for help and advice to avoid the Japanese trap.

Although the Allies were sympathetic, they did little to provide practical help. It is a generalisation to conclude that British resources were committed to theatres of war in Europe and the Middle East and they were preoccupied with the defence of Singapore. It is also easy to state that the Americans at this time were reluctant to enter into any war, either in Europe or South East Asia. Foreign Minister Direk Jayanama later revealed that the British minister Sir Josiah Crosby informed him that if Thailand resisted Japan's forces, Great Britain would offer maximum support. In the event, this promise did not transpire. This points in particular to the failure Operation Matador, in which British forces were being prepared to enter Thailand to defend against a Japanese attack. The operation was cancelled because it was considered that it would contravene the non-aggression pact signed in June 1940. It was a dubious decision that could have resulted in a far different outcome.

On 24 November 1941, the Japanese minister in Thailand approached the Thai government to inform them that for Japan to seize British territory, Japanese troops would need to land on Thai territory. He promised that this would not be an invasion but obviously it put Thailand into an invidious position. They wanted to defend their country but could not match the superiority of the Japanese forces. Luang Jayanama appealed to the Allies one final time, but they did not offer support. He told his cabinet colleagues; Great Britain and the United States have declared they would not fight therefore should Japan invade Thailand, it would difficult to hope for peace. The dark clouds of war were gathering in Thailand.

Time was running out. On 7 December 1941, in co-ordination with the attack on Pearl Harbour, the Japanese navy set sail westwards across the Gulf of Thailand. In the early evening Sir Josiah Crosby informed Luang Jayanama of the approaching armada. Luang Jayanama immediately tried to contact Prime Minister Luang Phibul with this devastating news but discovered he was in Battambong, about 200 miles east of Bangkok. Luang Jayanama informed the deputy prime minister, Luang Adun Adunyadetcarat. A short time later a Japanese delegation headed by the ambassador, Mr Tsubokami, arrived at the Thai government offices to request that the Japanese army be granted immediate *'right of free passage'* to enter Thailand. Decisions of this magnitude could not be made in the prime minister's absence. In an attempt to delay the inevitable, and based on his understanding that the matter was foreign policy business, Luang Adun asked Luang Jayanama to meet the delegation alone.

The delegation announced to Luang Jayanama that Japan had formally declared war on Great Britain and the United States in response to the constant barrage of pressure they had inflicted upon his country. Mr Tsubokami repeated the request that the Thai government allow the Japanese army to freely enter Thailand. Luang Jayanama responded by stating that Thailand's position in this war was neutral and they had no wish to support either side. He further reminded Mr Tsubokami that Thailand had already stated that it would resist aggression by any invading force, and only the prime minister could rescind this order. Mr Tsubokami set a deadline of 2am, after which the order would be given to land the army on Thai territory. Japan's troops were waiting off the coast of southern Thailand, and Thai forces were braced ready to fight a superior opponent.

An emergency cabinet meeting was called at 11pm to discuss the crisis, but they could not make any decisions until Luang Phibul returned. The Japanese did not wait and, at 2am in the morning of 8 December, their troops landed at Songkla, Pattani, Prachuap Khiri Khan, Nakhon Si Thammarat, Surat Thani and Bangphu. The Thai army and police force defended their positions valiantly in each of these small towns, but the pressure they sustained was intense and overwhelming. Casualties were inevitable.

Luang Phibul joined the cabinet meeting at 7am. He had already been briefed that Thailand was under attack. The cabinet agreed that resisting the Japanese infantry was futile and it was too late for Great Britain and United States to offer support.

Luang Phibul met Mr Tsubokami and listened to three propositions: firstly, that the Japanese merely wanted free passage; secondly, that he sign an alliance with Japan in return for which they offered to defend Thailand, and thirdly, that Thailand and Japan become formal allies in the war against Great Britain and the United States with a promise that Thailand would regain territories previously lost to Great Britain and France.

After deliberating the propositions, the cabinet agreed to accept the first proposal on the written undertaking that Japan would respect Thailand's independence, sovereignty and honour. The Japanese minister agreed, orders were despatched to end the fighting and a settlement on these terms was signed. The news was announced to an astonished public at 4:30 in the afternoon. Tragically, there had been loss of life amongst the Thai military, but it is to the honour of the Thai nation that they fought a superior army to defend their integrity and patriotism. Although the agreement would save Thailand from Japanese tyranny, it was far from popular within the cabinet and among the public. Almost immediately some ministers met to discuss how they could fight back and if it was possible to maintain contact the Allies.

Luang Phibul was trapped by a dilemma. He had previously welcomed Japanese ministrations and was receptive to their cause, but he knew that Thailand valued its neutrality above all else. Over several years the Japanese had gradually gained the upper hand but now they had revealed their true intention, which was to back the Thai government into a corner knowing that their military was inferior. Nor could the Allies help. Perhaps Luang Phibul felt his only option to save his country was to co-operate with the Japanese. But there is evidence that on 3 December 1941 he secretly agreed to allow the Japanese free passage in southern Thailand on condition they avoided Bangkok and central Thailand. There was also a provision for Thailand to regain territories ceded to Malaya in the south and Burma in the north. In the event, the agreement was either not accurately communicated or the Japanese had other ideas.

The New York Times reported that on 5 December, three days before the invasion, a large number of Japanese aeroplanes flew over Ubon. No bombs were dropped and there was no opposition, but people were disturbed. The report goes on to state that on 7 December thirty aeroplanes appeared, although it does not say if they landed. More than sixty Americans and 200 British citizens were trapped in Thailand when the borders were closed. As they departed they were treated with the utmost courtesy and respect by the Thai people, who were embarrassed by their prime minister's decision. Many people thought that Luang Phibul did not have any choice but to allow the Japanese the *'right of free passage'* to ensure that bloodshed was minimised.

Despite Japan agreeing not to enter Bangkok, more than 2,000 troops immediately made their camp at the Royal Bangkok Sports Club. *The New York Times* report asserts that the agreement forced the government to 'supply all facilities' to the Japanese, which included vehicles originally supplied by the United States.

Thailand's decision to allow free passage was a signal to the British and American governments that Thailand had, *de facto*, allied itself with the Japanese. This was verified by an additional agreement signed on 21 December in which Thailand and Japan each agreed to respect the independence and sovereignty of the other and committed to assist one another with political, military and economic support if either entered a conflict with a third country. They further agreed that neither country would enter a peace treaty or declare a truce without the consent of the other. Luang Direk Jayanama later wrote that he found a secret clause revealing that Japan would assist Thailand in regaining territories lost to Great Britain and, in return, Thailand would help Japan in the war against Great Britain and the United States. This new agreement superseded the agreement signed on 8 December.

The RAF began bombing military targets in the Bangkok area. The British legation in Thailand, Sir Josiah Crosby, justified the raids because Japan had declared war on Great Britain and the United States, and therefore their military bases throughout Thailand were legitimate targets. Predictably, the Japanese claimed that civilian installations were destroyed, which led Luang Phibul, supported by the Japanese, to claim that the raids were against international law. As a result, Thailand declared war on the Allies on 25 January 1942.

Although the United States did not formally accept the declaration, Great Britain, together with Australia and South Africa, acknowledged that a state of war existed. However, there was no intention to retaliate. As the war progressed, this declaration created considerable political and military difficulty for the Allies, particularly Great Britain, in responding positively to requests from Thailand's anti-Japanese guerrilla force, the Seri Thai.

Chapter 3

JAPANESE DETERMINATION

It took just seventy days for the Japanese armies to move through Malaya to capture Singapore. On the 15 February 1942, 130,000 Allied soldiers became Prisoners of War. The Japanese took over the administration of the island and brought with them their policy of eliminating ethnic groups that were suspected of holding anti-Japanese views and sentiments. In the 'Sook Ching' purge the Japanese Kempeitai targeted Chinese male residents between the ages of eighteen and fifty. Estimates of fatalities vary between 5,000 and 50,000.

Whilst preparing strategic plans to make inroads into South East Asia, the Japanese planned to maximise the use of existing railways especially between Bangkok and Singapore. But Burma was their key to advance further west, in particular towards India. Whilst Japan's navy had control of the sea, they could defend transportation from Singapore northwards through the Andaman Sea and Indian Ocean. But heavy losses and casualties at the battle of Midway in June 1942 severely reduced their naval power. They many lost ships and could not replace them quickly enough. They were in desperate need of an alternative route to provide support to their army in southern Burma and their ambitions to advance.

Japanese engineers had visited pre-war Thailand disguised as tourists to secretly survey potential routes for a railway between Thailand and Burma. They looked at a route from Kanchanaburi to Tavoy but more detailed surveys took place in February 1942. The conclusion was a recommendation to construct a railway between Nong Pladuk in Thailand (fifty miles due east of Bangkok) and Thanbyuzayat in Burma (250 miles further north).

It was an extremely ambitious plan and thought by many to be impossible. A serious lack of support transport for heavy machinery, virtually impassable roads and a very tight timescale made the task daunting. The Japanese forced vast numbers of Allied Prisoners of War held in Singapore into labour camps spread out along the proposed route. This was in contravention of the Geneva Convention, which outlawed any attempts to force Prisoners of War into working for their captors (amongst many other things). The Japanese blatantly failed to ratify the Convention. They believed that, on surrender, these men gave up their rights and allegiance to their country and could be put to any task demanded by their captors.

Furthermore, they enticed Asian civilians from Malaya, Indonesia, Burma and Thailand into labouring on the railway construction with promises of good working conditions, good pay and family accommodation. They became known as Romusha. Through no fault of their own, they had no leadership or organisational skills and no discipline. The atrocious conditions to which they were subjected resulted in a very high death rate from cholera, malaria and starvation.

In May 1942 groups of Allied Prisoners were sent to southern Burma to repair airfields before moving to Thanbyuzayat to commence construction of the railway from the Burmese side. Ubon Prisoner Thomas Whitehead was in that first group and remembers the train journey from Singapore to Georgetown in Malaya, where they were transferred onto a ship to sail to Moulmein. His ship was attacked by American B-24 Liberators and sustained some damage but, although they took on water, the voyage was completed.

These men were followed in June by a group of 3,000 Prisoners who left Singapore by train for Thailand. Thirty or more men were crammed into closed freight wagons together with their personal gear, unit supplies and Japanese stores. They were deprived of food, water and toilet facilities except, if they were lucky, when the train stopped to refuel. Upon arrival at Nong Pladuk one group was ordered to build stock yards to receive construction materials. A second group was moved two miles west to Ban Pong to prepare a transit camp. Then from October, during the monsoon season, Prisoners started to arrive at Nong Pladuk, many of them already in a desperate condition, and immediately forced to walk to Ban Pong where they were allocated to a work camp further up the route of the proposed railway line. Each camp turned into a quagmire from the incessant rain. They were depressing and miserable places clouded in deprivation, brutality and uncertainty. Many Prisoners were forced to walk for scores of miles alongside the river Kwai Noi through the jungle to remote camps.

Conditions deteriorated rapidly as the line progressed. Many Prisoners were already in poor physical shape when they arrived, but the work demanded of them drove them to exhaustion and poor health. There were no medical supplies to treat serious outbreaks of malaria, cholera, beriberi and ulcers, and insufficient food and nutrition to sustain them. The Japanese had no sympathy or respect for their fellow human beings. They demanded that the railway be completed at all costs, including life!

The most accurate figures are taken from Rod Beattie's book *Death Railway*. It records that a total of 239,711 Prisoners of War and Romusha were employed on the railway and estimates that 97,652 died; that is a death rate of over 40%, or two out of every five men. Out of 61,811 Allied Prisoners of War a total of 12,227 died; that is almost 20% or one in five Prisoners who died whilst working on the railway.

Remarkably, the railway was completed in October 1943. The north and south working parties met at Konkoita (160 miles from Nong Pladuk) in Northern Thailand. The Japanese immediately started to move troops and supplies into Burma whilst they transported their own sick and injured back towards Bangkok. Most of the Prisoners who were not so sick that they need hospital treatment were transferred to maintenance camps and kept busy repairing the railway after it collapsed or was bombed, or after derailments. Many men requiring hospital treatment were sent back to a hospital camp at Nong Pladuk.

The Japanese advanced through Burma and met the British army in north-east India at the bloody battles of Kohima and Imphal between April and July 1944. In arguably one of the greatest ever battles in British history, the Allied armies defeated the Japanese and forced them into retreat. One of the obvious and convenient routes to withdraw was along the railway. Others retreated along the northern route to Chiang Mai and then by train to Bangkok.

The Japanese demanded huge loans from the Thai government to finance their operations. Finance Minister Luang Direk Jayanama wrote that the Bank of Siam deposited 1,230,701,083 baht into the Yokohama Specie Bank between December 1941 and June 1945. The Japanese pegged the value of the Thai baht at par with the Japanese yen. This effectively meant that there was no true exchange rate for the yen during the war. Using the post-war Bretton exchange rate of 360 yen to US$1 to estimate of the value of the loans, it roughly converts to US$3.4 million at 1949 values. This is approximately US$ 47.6 million at 2018 values, which is approximately £35.5 million. The effect on the Thai economy was devastating as the cost of living increased fourfold in six years.

Further demands for finance from the Japanese were resisted. This heightened tension and, with Japan's increasingly precarious situation in the war, there was a distinct possibility that the Japanese would take over the entire administration of the Thai government. Although the Japanese lacked skills of administration in foreign countries, they took control in French Indochina in March 1945 to avoid the French retaking power as Hitler faced defeat in Europe. The same could have happened in Thailand but the situation was changing rapidly. Throughout the time the Japanese were 'guests' of the Thai government, the Seri Thai resistance movement had grown and they had contacted former Allies of Great Britain and the United States to discuss plans to attack the Japanese.

Chapter 4

THAI RESISTANCE

Opinion on Prime Minister Luang Phibul's decision to allow the Japanese the *'right of free passage'* over Thai territory was divided. There were those who concluded that, with no realistic defences, he had to avoid serious loss of life against the overwhelming Japanese incursion; there were also those who suspected he had a more than generous amount of sympathy with their aggressive strategy.

In the event, the Japanese entered Thailand without receiving permission. Fighting broke out at the coastal towns of Songkla, Pattani, Prachuap Khiri Khan, Nakhon Si Thammarat, Surat Thani and Bangphu and inland at Phatthalung and Samut Songkhram. Unfortunately there was loss of life on both sides before the ceasefire was communicated. Japanese military forces were established in Thailand and most Thai people were unhappy with the situation.

There followed a government re-shuffle in which Luang Pridi, a known Japanese opponent, was moved sideways to the eminent position of Prince Regent. This was still a prestigious role but one in which his influence in government matters was greatly reduced, although it did allow him time and space to secretly initiate and develop the Seri Thai Movement. He was a natural leader with considerable political skill, which he drew from his experience as a lawyer and protagonist of the 1932 coup d'état and architect of the resulting new constitution.

On 11 December 1941, shortly after the Japanese entered Thailand, Luang Pridi held a secret meeting with his most trusted political colleagues to discuss plans to organise a plausible and credible resistance movement. He found the support and formed what was called the XO Group. They agreed it was pointless to think that the Thai military forces were equal to the Japanese, and they accepted the Allies had withdrawn support following Thailand's decision to assist Japan. That said, Luang Pridi proposed four objectives for the XO Group: to reduce the power and influence of Luang Phibul's government and policies with Japan; to encourage sabotage tactics on Japanese targets; to promote propaganda campaigns, and, most importantly, to make urgent contact with the Allies to propose mutual support.

This latter objective received a severe setback in January 1942 when Thailand declared war on Great Britain and the United States. With a state of war existing with their former Allies, the XO Group could not realistically expect them to readily support their cause. It was going to be a most difficult task to convince the Allies, but they were certain that collaboration was the only plausible way to defeat the Japanese.

The XO Group would only allow the most trustworthy to join its ranks and therefore its expansion was slow and methodical. Even so, the majority of Thailand's population openly resented the Japanese, which gave the Group the optimism and encouragement that, in time, an effective internal resistance movement could be established.

The XO Group's most critical problem was establishing secret communications with a trusted Allied source. Apart from the obvious technical issues, there was little chance of opening a secret 'diplomatic' dialogue with either the government of Great Britain or the United States. The Group hoped that Thais living or studying abroad would form their own resistance movements rather than returning to a Thailand influenced by Japan. They further hoped that these groups would try to contact Allied governments to persuade them of their cause, and create military or clandestine channels to attempt to contact the XO Group. Once contact was established the XO Group could meet the Allies to impress upon them that they were dealing with the right people and open up the possibility of effective resistance activity against the Japanese. It was a highly ambitious plan but they had high hopes of achieving success.

Fortunately, events abroad moved quickly. On the 25 January 1942 Thailand delivered its declaration of war on the United States to the Swiss consul in Bangkok. There is uncertainty whether the diplomatic process that followed was correctly undertaken; certainly the story is contentious. The Thai Minister in Washington DC at the time was M. R. Seni Pramoj. He was the great grandson of Thailand's King Rama II who ruled Thailand from 1809 to 1824. (The prefix M.R. means 'Mom Rajawongse' and indicates his relationship to the monarchy.) When the Japanese landed, he publicly declared his opposition to his government's decision to allow them the right of free passage. In an emotional statement he informed the Thai government that he would *'carry out only orders which, in my opinion, are of His Majesty's Government's free will.'*

Reports suggest that the Thai government sent the declaration of war on the United States to M.R. Seni Pramoj at the Thai embassy in Washington DC with instructions for him to deliver it to the US government. The common assertion is that he failed to deliver the declaration to the American government by deliberately keeping it in his pocket. Whether this is true is open to debate. Why would the Thai government request that any document, especially a declaration of war, be delivered to M.R. Seni Pramoj and expect him to act on behalf of the Thai government when he had publicly and vehemently denounced their decision to allow the Japanese into Thailand? In addition, Luang Pridi stated that under international protocol the declaration was considered delivered to the United States once it had been received by the Swiss Consul in Bangkok. Therefore, there was no further need to involve M.R. Seni Pramoj. Furthermore, there is no record in the US State Department of any meeting between any of their officials and M.R. Seni Pramoj to discuss the declaration.

The conclusion is that he dramatised the effect of his opposition to the Thai government, and Luang Phibul in particular, to impress the Americans. What can be established is that the Swiss Consul delivered the declaration to the State Department on 2

February 1942. However, the United States chose to ignore it because they would *'not dignify the action of the present Japanese-controlled government of Thailand by a formal declaration of war.'*

In a postscript to this controversy, Luang Pridi, in his position as Prince Regent, was required under Thai law to sign the declaration on behalf of Thailand's young king, who was in Switzerland furthering his education. In fact, Luang Pridi made himself absent from Bangkok to purposely avoid signing the declaration. This effectively left the declaration without any legal basis.

However, a state of war existed between the United States and Japan and all diplomatic channels in Bangkok had been promptly closed. Many diplomatic staff were interred, potentially to be deported at a later date. The Swiss Consul in Bangkok undertook to communicate between Thailand, Great Britain and the United States but, as the war progressed, this arrangement was apparently not all that successful.

Thailand's action unsettled the one hundred or so Thai nationals, who were mainly students, living in the United States. They faced an uncomfortable dilemma: if they returned to their families in Thailand, the Japanese would suspect they were spies, but if they stayed in the United States their bursaries would probably stop and they anticipated a hostile reaction from the American authorities and public. However, most of them decided to remain rather than face an uncertain future from the Japanese. They contacted M.R. Seni Pramoj for advice. He organised them into a resistance group, which he hoped the Americans would train to infiltrate Thailand and make contact with anti-Japanese groups to obtain intelligence. M.R. Seni Pramoj was not in contact with Luang Pridi, but he was certain that someone in an influential position within Thailand would seek to initiate an internal resistance force.

He took his idea to the Americans. Everyone realised that sending western agents into Thailand was futile because, without

Asian features and with little command of the Thai language, they would be easily recognised. Following successful negotiations with the newly formed Office of Strategic Services (OSS), a special unit called the Seri Thai (Free Thai) was formed. They were independent of any United States military force. Training began with physical conditioning, followed by the use of guerrilla tactics and intelligence gathering techniques. They were being prepared to infiltrate Thailand at the appropriate time.

In Great Britain, the delivery of the declaration to the government was as farcical as the events in the United States. Thailand's representative in London was Luang Bhadaravadi. He was not as demonstrative in his opposition to the Japanese presence as his counterpart in Washington DC, but also he did not agree with Luang Phibul's decision. In a letter to Luang Pridi dated 4 April 1978, he confirmed that he first heard the news that Thailand had declared war on Great Britain from a BBC radio broadcast. He did not recollect receiving any communication from the Thai government, nor did he recall the minister, Phra Manuvat, delivering any such document to the British Foreign Office.

Nevertheless, the British government received the declaration, presumably through the Swiss embassy; unlike the United States, however, they immediately declared Thailand as an enemy of the state. They took no further action, although they were very angry with Thailand for allowing the Japanese through their country, which eventually led to the loss of the colonies of Malaya, Singapore and Burma. The British government made it clear that they would demand compensation for these losses but for now, coupled with the escalating war in Europe, it was enough to accept the declaration and relegate it to the side lines.

There were a few Thai nationals in Britain, many of whom were students attending British universities. They found themselves facing the same uncomfortable dilemma about whether to return to Thailand and face Japanese oppression, or remain in England with the threat of being ostracised. None of them accepted their government's decision to accommodate the Japanese, and they repudiated the declaration of war on the Allies. They formed themselves into a group with the same intentions as their fellow countrymen in the United States. However, the British government was understandably not too keen on supporting a resistance movement from a country with which they were at war. The Thais were unknown, unarmed, untrained and overseen by non-military personnel.

Charles Cruikshank in his book *SOE in the Far East* quotes Anthony Eden as saying: '*but here we are having dealings with a (Thai) government or creature that collaborates with the Japs* [sic] *as a head of the government (Phibul). This don't seem to make political sense and I have a pretty clear view that the War Cabinet would feel as I do.*' He was right: how could Britain co-operate and support a loose organisation of unknown individuals, purporting to be allies from a country with which they were at war?

Nevertheless, the British government allowed the Thai expats to join the Pioneer Corps. This was the only military unit in which enemy aliens were allowed to enlist. The duties of the Pioneer Corp were menial but necessary. The Thai recruits were unfairly branded as enemy aliens. Many German and Austrian nationals, typically from the Jewish community, had escaped from the Nazi regime and joined the Pioneer Corp to fight back. The SOE took an interest in enemy aliens as potential saboteurs and intelligence gatherers. They identified thirty-seven Thais to train as spies and agents.

Communication between the group in the United States and the one in Great Britain was established but there was a serious lack of communication between the offices of the OSS and SOE. This was as much to do with political differences as their military competitiveness. But, with no serious political constraints to hold them back, the OSS steamed ahead with their plans to train their Thai agents with a view to finding and contacting any internal resistance movement within Thailand.

PART TWO

THE PRISONERS
MOVE TO UBON

Chapter 5

A TOWN CALLED UBON

Ubon is located in the north east of Thailand close to the borders of Thailand, Laos and Cambodia. It lies on the river Mun about 350 miles east of Bangkok. In the nineteenth century Ubon grew as a convenient trading centre mainly because of its location. Travel by road before the War was difficult, which made the river a lifeline for transport and trade between the scores of villages along its course. By any standards, the river Mun is a long and wide river that flows into the Mekong some forty-five miles to the east.

Khun Nikom, is a lifelong resident of Phibun Mangsahan, which is thirty miles east of Ubon, and at one time he was the village leader. He remembers his 1940s' childhood when he spent idyllic days playing with his friends by the river. He watched the wood-burning steamboats picking up passengers, produce and livestock at the pier in the morning prior to sailing to Ubon's riverside markets.

The roads in Ubon and beyond were nothing more than well-trodden tracks beaten down into a rusty-red laterite soil. In the rainy season travel was hampered by the monsoon floods, which left quagmires and made travel difficult if not impossible. In the 1930s, motorised vehicle transport was rare and the buffalo and cart was the only transport available. News, business and communications between the major towns, and especially with Bangkok, travelled slowly if at all.

Surprisingly, it was the arrival of aviation that first brought Ubon a little closer to Bangkok. In January 1911, French aviator Charles Van Den Born landed a Henry Farman biplane at the Bangkok Sports Club in the centre of the city to demonstrate the wondrous capabilities of flight. His skill captivated Thailand's royal family and its government. They instantly recognised its commercial potential, whilst officers of the armed forces had the vision to recognise the military possibilities. An aviation programme, including aircraft manufacture, was started and a base established at Don Muang, north of Bangkok. Don Muang played a significant role in World War Two and later became Bangkok's International airport. It is now Bangkok's second airport after Suvanabhumi; it remains the headquarters for the Royal Thai Air Force.

The development of civilian aviation benefited Ubon. In June 1921, a serious epidemic of cholera broke out and the local authority sent an urgent request to the Public Health Department in Bangkok for medicine and medical staff. The journey by road would have taken two weeks but on 21 June an aeroplane flew from Don Muang and arrived in Ubon three hours later. The advantages of receiving this urgently needed help were obvious, and decisions were quickly made to bring aviation to the north east of Thailand. In the spring of the following year, the Royal Aeronautical Service staged an air display at Ubon to promote its proposed regular air mail service between the major towns in north-east Thailand and Bangkok.

Having reaped the benefits of flight during the cholera epidemic, the generous people of Ubon contributed to the purchase of five new aircraft and the construction of an airstrip and hangars. A few months later, on 1 June 1922, a Breguet 14s aircraft landed at Ubon and a regular postal service between Bangkok, Korat, Roi Et and Ubon began.

There was further excitement in Ubon when, on 11 June 1924, a Portuguese owned De Havilland DH9 aircraft landed on the airfield. It had just completed the twenty-first leg of an adventurous long-distance flight from Lisbon in Portugal to Macau on the east coast of China near Hong Kong. This epic flight was a preparation for a later attempt to fly round the world.

Travel and communication to Bangkok was enhanced further when, in 1930, the railway line was extended from Korat to create a continuous link between Bangkok and Ubon. It was the same railway used by the POWs to travel to Ubon and is still used frequently today. Although the journey times were slow, it boosted trade and commerce and added to Ubon's growing importance as a regional centre.

During this period, a significant army garrison was established in Ubon to monitor and safeguard the border with French Indochina along the river Mekong to the east. The Royal Thai Air Force was not permanently based at Ubon in the pre-war period but squadrons were moved to airfields whenever conflict was anticipated so they could respond promptly to any call to action.

Chapter 6

THE JAPANESE WANT
AN AIRSTRIP AT UBON

The records are unclear on the reasons why the Japanese wanted to build an airstrip at Ubon but there are several theories. In August 1944, Prime Minister Luang Phibul was replaced by Luang Khuang Aphaiwong. He secretly supported the Seri Thai and was a close confident of Luang Pridi, but he was able to conceal this from the Japanese. The Seri Thai was strengthened by the co-operation of the Royal Thai armed forces and the police, who were now working with them throughout the country.

At the end of 1944, Japan was facing two issues: the reality of military defeat following the battles at Kohima and Imphal, and a confident new Thai government that was standing up to the pressing financial demands of the Japanese army. In addition, unbeknown to the Japanese, the Seri Thai Movement under the leadership of Luang Pridi had successfully contacted the Allies and was receiving substantial physical support from the SOE and OSS. More branches of the Seri Thai Movement were being established throughout Thailand, and the north east of Thailand was particularly strong. Vital intelligence was being gathered for the SOE and OSS and they began to train guerrillas in several secret camps throughout the country.

An OSS report dated 29 May 1945 details the Thai government's resistance to the Japanese. Although this report was written when the Ubon airstrip was well under construction, it gives an insight into the government's growing dissent:

The Thai government had demonstrated:
Refusal of (one) hundred-million-baht credit in May 1945.

Refusal of a request in May (1945) for Japanese control of roads and railways in Thailand.
Denial of Thai arsenals at Ban Mah and Bong Prab to the Japanese.
Refusal of the use of the Sattahib weather station and exploitation of the eastern shores of the Gulf of Thailand.
Denial of many of the Japanese requests for 'reserved areas.' This refusal is usually achieved by moving in elements of the Thai army. Their presence is then used as an excuse for denying these areas to the Japanese. Recent events in Korat are a case in point.

The report continues with factual evidence of how the Thai government was co-operating with the Allies:

Assisting the Air Forces by exfiltrating downed crews.
Concealing Allied operators in the heart of Bangkok and high-ranking government officials holding daily briefings with them.
Willingness of Thai military and political officials to attend planning meetings.
Established an intelligence network with direct contact to OSS HQ in Ceylon (Sri Lanka) with Thai operators in eleven cities outside of Bangkok.
Willingness to allow OSS and SOE officers to lead Seri Thai groups.

The report quotes a revealing communication from Luang Pridi (date and recipient not recorded, but likely to have been sent to OSS command in the same period):

'As the American authorities have often warned us not to take premature action against the Japanese, the Thai Resistance Movement has always borne this warning in mind. But at present I believe that if the Resistance Movement comes into the open Thailand will be in a position to further weaken the Japanese will to fight. It will be the disintegration in the so-called Co-Prosperity Sphere and will consequently compel the Japanese to accept more quickly the terms of unconditional surrender to the Allies. On the other hand, it was suggested that the Resistance Movement should try to obstruct every facility the Japanese may

41

ask of us. We have complied with this request. You are well aware that the Japanese are increasingly suspicious. Recently the Thai government refused a Japanese demand for an increased credit of 100,000,000 baht. The present government has also expressed to me their intention of resigning if the Japanese insist in this matter. In that case a new government will have to be formed and take measures against the Japanese by declaring void all debts and agreements the Phibul government concluded with the Japanese. This includes the treaty concerning the incorporation of the four Malayan states and the Shan state in Thailand, as well as the declaration of war against the United States and Great Britain. Relations between Thailand and the two above mentioned countries will thus be established on a basis prior to 8 December 1941. Before carrying out these measures, I wish to keep you "au courant". I am convinced of the United States' good intentions towards Thailand's independence and of its sincere sympathy for the Thai people. I believe that if the United States officially confirmed the independence of Thailand on the day when we take action and considered Thailand not as an enemy but as a member of the United Nations, it would greatly strengthen the Thai people, who are prepared for any sacrifice in any case. I have informed the Supreme Commander of the South East Asia Command in the same sense.'

The Japanese military command in Thailand had to react. Their power was weakening and there was growing hostility from Thailand's civilians, who simply wanted the Japanese to leave. But they were facing defeat in the wider theatre of war. Surrender was not option for the Japanese. They would defend their positions by whatever means against the background of growing resistance. They decided to build airstrips at Phetchaburi (south west of Bangkok), Lampang (south of Chiang Mai) and Ubon. The exact reasons for these decisions are not known but there are four postulations relative to Ubon.

First: from the beginning of the Japanese subjugation, the Thai government was coerced into lending money to finance their war effort. In 1945 the Thai government refused to advance a further

100,000,000 baht because the Japanese had reneged on the contracted terms and previous loans had not been repaid. If the government did resign, as Luang Pridi expressed in his letter, a new administration would be compelled to declare all previous agreements and policies with Japan since 8 December 1941 null and void. In theory, the Japanese troops would have to leave Thailand because the government would withdraw its permission allowing them to stay in Thailand. Japan would not accept this and could possibly retaliate by declaring a state of war on Thailand at worst, or taking over the Thai government at best.

The Japanese had always been reluctant to take over the administration of any country fully because they did not have enough capable and experienced civil servants to manage acquired territories. This was the case in French Indochina, where they allowed the Vichy French incumbents to continue administering their own affairs but retained the upper hand. However, when the Vichy French government was dissolved in the summer of 1944 after France was liberated following the defeat of Hitler's Germany by the Allies, the Japanese became apprehensive and no longer trusted French Indochina's governor, General Decoux. When he refused to hand over control of his troops and communications, the Japanese responded by declaring a state of martial law. They ordered the government to close its borders with Thailand and arrest all French and Indochinese residents, but the government refused to comply.

Given these events in a country adjoining Thailand, it is possible that the Japanese were contemplating a similar course of action. If the Japanese were to declare a state of martial law in Thailand, arguably they needed defensive positions to quell the civil unrest that would inevitably break out throughout the country. Thousands of Japanese troops were being relocated to north-east Thailand and French Indochina, possibly in readiness to react if a decision was taken to take over the administration government of Thailand. An additional airstrip at Ubon would put the Japanese in a good position to assist in counteracting any uprising in the region.

Second: perhaps counter-intuitive to the threat of martial law, the Allied victories at Imphal and Kohima initiated the threat of impending defeat on the Japanese, and they were considering retreating towards the east. Japanese survivors from these decisive battles pulled back through Thailand, using the Thailand-Burma railway as one of their escape routes.

It is logical to suggest that the Japanese considered withdrawing further east to the relative safety of French Indochina by using the existing rail link between Bangkok and Ubon. Intelligence reports suggested that the Japanese may have been planning a new line of communication from French Indochina along the line between Ubon and Bangkok. Speculation implies that this might have originated from Pakse, which is just over eighty miles due east from Ubon, but further intelligence stated that the Japanese might consider taking the road north from Ubon either to Mukdahan, where they could cross the river Mekong to Savvanakhet, or further north to Nakhon Phanom, where they could cross to Thakhek. However, the Japanese were known to be facing a serious deterioration of their motor transport and a shortage of fuel.

Further evidence can be found in another report recording that it was 'worth noting' that traffic from Bangkok to the French Indochina border was about seventy to eighty tons per day, consisting of mainly troops, military stores and equipment. The report concluded that: *what conclusion is to be drawn from this it is hard to say. Traffic in the opposite direction seems to be small.* An airstrip at Ubon would have provided defensive cover for retreat.

Third: although Ubon already had an existing aerodrome, and it was occasionally used by both the Japanese and Royal Thai Air Forces, a second and more remote airstrip could be guarded more effectively.

There is some truth in the reasoning that local Ubon people were spying on the Japanese and passing intelligence through the Seri Thai agents to the Allies. It is also very likely that the Japanese knew that the Allies had identified the existing aerodrome, and this raised concerns about potential bombing raids. However, Allied aircraft did not have the range to fly heavy bombers to Ubon, complete a raid and return to their bases in India or Ceylon. The payload of heavy bombs was too great for the amount fuel required to make the long return journey. It was unlikely that the Japanese were aware of the Allied plans to launch co-ordinated attacks on Japanese positions in South East Asia, including Thailand with the help of the Seri Thai. But if they were, they would have realised they needed strong defences. The Seri Thai in north-east Thailand were a growing fighting force and had to be continually restrained by the SOE.

Fourth: it has been postulated that, had the Allies advanced into Thailand from the west, the Japanese would have held their defence line at Korat and the Petchabun mountain range, which runs to the north of Korat. If that were the case, an airfield at Ubon would have provided support to the defending Japanese army.

Whatever the reasoning behind their decision to build an airstrip at Ubon, there is no doubt that it was strategically well placed for the Japanese to react. Neither was there any doubt that Allied Prisoners of War were going to build it. The men were slowly transferred to the village of Ban Nong Phai, about six miles north of Ubon town centre. This area was relatively flat and, although north-east Thailand endured a heavy monsoon rainfall, it was not seriously affected by flooding. This meant, in theory at least, that the airstrip would be operational throughout the year and, if constructed properly, in most weather conditions.

The high-handed Japanese had no sympathy for the welfare and way of life of the villagers of Ban Nong Phai. Although the land did not actually belong to the villagers outright (actually it was owned by the government and they leased it to the villagers), it was theirs to farm as they wished. Nevertheless, the governor of Ubon, the officers of the Thai Army, Air Force or Police did not have any powers to stop the Japanese riding roughshod through the village.

Chapter 7

MOVING TO UBON

After the Thailand-Burma railway was completed, many Prisoners found themselves in maintenance camps strung along the length of the railway. They still endured harsh and difficult conditions. There was little improvement in food, and access to decent medical supplies was virtually non-existent. Many of those not in maintenance camps returned to large camps at Nong Pladuk at the start of the railway.

One well-respected officer at Nong Pladuk was Colonel Phillip Toosey of 135 Field Regiment Royal Artillery. He maintained strict discipline, cleanliness and hygiene amongst his men and refused separate officers' accommodation. He encouraged sabotage, delay tactics and did not stand in the way of escape attempts, providing the risks were fully understood.

Nong Pladuk camp expanded to hold about 8,000 Prisoners and, despite the huge numbers of men, conditions were reported to be generally better than in most of the camps further along the railway. Alongside the camp was a huge depot with sidings for trains and stores holding supplies to be transported up the line. However, with an improved flow of intelligence from the Seri Thai, Nong Pladuk became a target for Allied bombing raids. Sadly, the intelligence did not separate Japanese targets from the areas in which the Prisoners were accommodated, and they were hit by friendly fire. Despite constant requests from the Prisoners, the Japanese refused them permission to dig slit trenches and build shelters in which they could take cover during the raids. It was during one particularly heavy raid on 7 September 1944, that almost one hundred Prisoners were killed and 400 injured.

The raids continued into 1945, thankfully with fewer casualties, although the hospital and cookhouse were destroyed, adding to the men's discomfort. Whilst the raids created apprehension amongst the Prisoners their morale rose as the Japanese did not respond with anti-aircraft fire, which gave the Allies the upper hand. Following their defeat in Burma there was a steady increase in the number of Japanese troops retreating on the railway through Nong Pladuk towards Bangkok. They were anxious and agitated, and there was a growing suspicion that they would retaliate against the Prisoners.

Despite the increase in tension, the Prisoners continued to take imaginative risks to sabotage trains passing through Nong Pladuk. A popular trick was to put gritty soil in an axle grease box. However, some trains were carrying Japanese sick and injured and their own medical staff were not providing them with adequate care or treatment. Remarkably, some sympathetic Prisoners risked severe personal punishment by giving them food and water from their own meagre rations. (These acts of compassion are featured in the beautiful 'Humanitas' stained glass artwork by Gerry Cummins and Jill Stehn in the Thailand-Burma Railway Centre in Kanchanaburi.)

As 1944 drew to a close, the Japanese relocated Allied officers, including Colonel Toosey, to Nakhon Nayok. The change in routine unsettled some of the Prisoners but it was not long before many were relocated to other work camps, including Ubon.

The first group began their journey to Ubon in February 1945. A secret message from the Swiss Consul in Bangkok, dated 27 February 1945, stated that 1,000 Prisoners had passed through Bangkok from the south and were probably continuing the journey by rail in the direction of Indochina. Although it does not mention Ubon by name, it is probable this was the first batch of Ubon men. The report continued that the men were dressed in shorts or trousers and had shoes, but only half of them had shirts. Some were smoking, and most were wearing hats.

Other groups of various sizes travelled in the following months up to the end of May. Their journey started by train from Nong Pladuk towards Bangkok. Some of the men nervously shared their journey with Japanese troops returning from Burma who were weary, with a tell-tale look of defeat imprinted on their faces. Their uniforms were falling apart at the seams from the unrelenting tropical conditions and climate. They were exhausted and morale was low; their fate, just like that of the Prisoners, was uncertain. Despite shared fears, the two groups were kept apart. The Japanese travelled in the passenger wagons at the front of the train whilst the Prisoners, as in times before, were confined to the cramped goods wagons at the back.

The trains terminated at Thonburi on the west bank of the river Chao Phraya, which runs through the centre of Bangkok. At the Thonburi jetty the Prisoners were transferred onto barges or even sampans to travel the eight miles or so down river to Khlong Toei in the Port of Bangkok. Some vessels were unstable, with as many as forty men in a single boat. They were packed under tarpaulin covers, cowering in vain attempts to fight off vicious mosquitoes. As they sailed down the river inevitably some of the boats took water onboard. It was panic stations as they transferred to other vessels, which was a highly dangerous manoeuvre on the deep, fast-flowing waters.

As they sailed down river, they passed some of Bangkok's finest buildings, including the Grand Palace and magnificent Wat Arun, which today are amongst Bangkok's iconic tourist attractions. They saw people walking on the streets and traffic moving freely through the city; after three years of incarceration along the Thailand-Burma railway, this reminded them of their isolation in another world. Harold Churchill recalls passing under a bomb-damaged bridge with its span pointing into the sky like '*awkward blessings*', and Fergus Anckorn wrote that he wished he could swap his uncertain future for the wonderous sights that he was passing through.

Once they arrived at Khlong Toei, they were housed in shabby dockland warehouses called go-downs. Unfortunately, the go-downs, railway tracks and stations of Bangkok were legitimate targets for Allied bombing raids. Following their harrowing experiences at Nong Pladuk, the men were understandably just as concerned and nervous that they might be caught up again in 'friendly fire'. Some of them were kept in the go-downs for a few days, whilst train transport to Ubon was organised. Regular delays arose from waiting for a serviceable train or repair to the track between Bangkok and Korat following bomb damage. Other groups had to stay longer to work in nearby oil refineries and warehouses.

Thomas Whitehead, an American Prisoner who was later transferred to Ubon, remembers staying there for several weeks. He said the overcrowded conditions were awful, and exercise or movement outside the buildings was often forbidden. They occupied their time by taking every opportunity to sabotage Japanese equipment or steal useful items from the warehouses. Unlike previous camps, the go-downs were located in a built-up industrial area away from local habitation, which reduced the opportunities to barter for extra food to supplement their meagre diets.

Other groups of men were allowed to dig slit trenches about 250 yards from their go-down. It was a concession they were thankful for when in March, not long after they had prepared the trenches, the Allies delivered two heavy bombing raids, with reported damage and casualties. Thomas remembers that they sheltered in the slit trenches, but a warehouse storing raw rubber and other materials was destroyed and the resulting fire burned for about two weeks. He brings to mind that lives would have been lost without the slit trenches. But, once again, their spirits were lifted as they witnessed the unsuccessful efforts of the Japanese in bringing down the Allied bombers.

As the frequency of the raids increased, Thomas noted that the Allies must have been gaining the upper hand. The groups that stayed in the go-downs only for a few days were kept under close guard and not allowed outside. Understandably, their sense of fear from bombing raids was intensified because they had no refuge away from the target buildings.

Eventually the men moved on to Ubon. Gunner Tom Brown and Charles Steel both recall their particular groups being herded onto a train standing in the go-down sidings at short notice. Charles remembers his wagon had previously been used to transport oil and tar. Forty-four men were crammed into each wagon and they moved slowly along the few miles north to the main line, where they were transferred onto another train at the start of their long journey to Ubon. Whilst Charles and his group were waiting, an air raid took place; he recalls that they ran from the train onto an open lawn in front of a school. There was nowhere else to go.

Passing through Bangkok gave the POWs a chance to surreptitiously discover news about the progress of the war in the Far East and Europe. Private Hugh King Ashby recalls that he was in one of the last groups and was travelling through Bangkok in the back of a Japanese military truck. As the truck stopped at a junction, a Danish male civilian on a bicycle drew alongside and quietly told the men that 'the war in Europe was over'. Unfortunately, the Japanese guards overheard the conversation, although they did not understand what was being said. Suspicions were raised and the truck was diverted to a nearby Kempeitai station.

The Kempeitai were noted for extreme methods of torture and understandably the men became very apprehensive about the reception they were about to receive. They were taken to a room and ordered to keep silent. The Dane was taken to an adjoining room, where he was interviewed. The men were pleasantly surprised when, through the paper-thin walls, they heard the Kempeitai officer demand that the Dane tell them what he had said to the Prisoners. He replied, 'Good day and how are all of you?' Hearing this, the men had the perfect response to the same question when it was their turn to be interrogated! It was a remarkable escape from the notoriously aggressive Kempeitai.

Between late February and early May 1945, just over 3,000 men made the journey through Bangkok to Ubon. Travelling so far east and further away from the other camps naturally filled them with apprehension. Even though they had received occasional encouraging news about the progress of the war from well-meaning civilians, they did not have the means to verify such claims. They did not want to become over optimistic and build up their hopes that there might be an imminent end to their captivity. On the other hand, they feared they might be forgotten as they were so far away from the main camps in the west. As they arrived on the opposite side of the country, each Prisoner had his own thoughts about what the nervous and potentially trigger-happy Japanese soldiers might do to them.

The train journey was arduous. A report on Japanese troop movements dated 24 February 1945 stated:

The Thai government is being forced to accede to Japanese demands for increased rail transportation from Bangkok to Ubon. Thirty-five freight cars with a capacity of about 300 tons will be provided for each trip. The train will leave Bangkok every other day at 02:00 hours local time, arriving at Korat at 13:55 hours and in Ubon at 04:00 hours the next morning. On the return trip the train will leave Ubon at 17:00 hours and arrive in Bangkok at 20:00 hours the following day. The first train left Bangkok on 17 February.

That is a demanding one-way journey of at least twenty-six hours. A further report, dated 13 June 1945, reveals that trains to Ubon left Bangkok at 00:20 hours each Tuesday and Friday. They arrived in Korat at 14:20 hours and set off again at 15:40, with an expected arrival time in Ubon of 04:00 hours. Typically, each train had thirty passenger and box cars and made long stops at Ban Pachi junction, Ban Kong Khoi, Pak Chong, Lanchi and Sisaket, probably to take on more water and wood for fuel.

Allied air raids targeted the central railway workshop at Makasan in the centre of Bangkok. The bombers could reach Korat; on the 28 February 1945, they destroyed a bridge at Ban Mah, which severely affected the sidings at Korat and resulted in a line closure whilst repairs were carried out. This meant that the Prisoners were held in the go downs at Bangkok for longer than expected and was one reason why their arrival in Ubon was spread over a period of several weeks. Note also that many trains were damaged beyond repair as a result of Allied air raids and that maintenance was affected due to lack of spare parts. The result was a national crisis in the availability of train services. By early 1945 almost half of Thailand's trains were out of service and most diesel trains had been stopped because of fuel shortages.

Moving out of Bangkok, the Prisoners would have seen the homes of city dwellers on the edge of the track. These were homes occupied by people who were free but imprisoned by poverty.

The trains were fuelled by wood-burning engines and wound their way slowly through the suburbs until they reached Bangkok's airport at Don Muang. What did the POWs think when they saw the combined activities of the Japanese and Royal Thai Air Forces? Although they did not know it then, the next time they would see Don Muang would be when they were on their long journey home.

They travelled into a countryside dominated by tropical forests and vegetation with occasional rice fields. Arriving at Ayutthaya, the men were unaware that they were passing through the old capital of Thailand, which was to become a UNESCO World Heritage site in 1992. Its ancient temples were hidden from their view as they trundled through this historical Thai city.

Gradually the trains crossed more open plains, passing through villages to reach the small town of Saraburi. If they were lucky, they caught a glimpse of Saraburi's Buddhist temples. Moving further east, the train frequently stopped to take on more wood and water. These stops gave the Prisoners a brief respite, whilst brave Thai villagers risked punishment by giving them food and water. The Prisoners also took a risk by accepting the food.

By 1945, most of the Thai people had run out patience with the Japanese and resented their presence. They showed sympathy and compassion towards the Prisoners. They had a welcoming and natural beaming smile and an inherent curiosity that led them to stare at Europeans, in many cases for the first time. Despite the language barrier, attempts were made to pass on news about the status of the war, with hints about the likelihood defeating the Japanese. Predictably the Japanese guards reacted angrily and forcibly dispersed the villagers away from the train.

Once the journey restarted, the Prisoners travelled through more beautiful and colourful countryside with distant mountains and rivers. There were tiny settlements and villages with packs of barking dogs of mixed varieties and temperaments, snarling and snapping at the train as it passed through.

The next large town was Korat, which is known today as Nakhon Ratchasima. Korat was occupied by a large force of Japanese soldiers and just within reach of Allied bombers from Ceylon and India. Liberators flew unopposed at low levels to dispatch their bomb loads. The bombs were 370, 500 or 1,000 pounds and in total 340 were dropped, causing extensive damage. On one occasion a train carrying Prisoners stopped abruptly at Korat because of a bomb-damaged bridge. The men had to walk across its precarious timbers to the station, beyond which they spent the night waiting for another train to arrive from Ubon to allow them to continue their journey. As daylight dawned, they looked back at the precarious bridge and realised how lucky they had been not to fall into the river.

East of Korat is the region known as Issan. This was a poor economic region dependent on subsistence agriculture. Almost every family had land on which they grew rice between June and December and let their cattle graze over it in the months between. Growing rice in 1945 was labour intensive and backbreaking work. In June, with the arrival of the first monsoon rains, the sun-baked land was ploughed by driving a buffalo fitted with a crude wooden plough through the water-logged soil. The whole family worked together to bed out the individual roots of the rice plants. Although rice depends on water to grow and flourish, excessive monsoon rains can result in serious flooding and cause the plants to drown, creating a devastating crop failure. Equally, not enough monsoon rain could cause a drought. Harvesting the crop at exactly the right time required expert skill achieved through years of farming. The family gathered together again, cut the plants with sharp sickles and laid them out in bundles. After the bundles were collected, the grains were separated and laid out to dry in the hot sun. The rice was then ready to be stored but, before it was eaten the husk was separated to reveal the white kernel.

The Prisoners' trains passed through the Issan countryside between February and May, during the dormant season. At this time the rice fields were just grey stubble with buffalos and cows grazing, probably tended by a sleepy child whose daily task it was to watch over the family livestock. It would be very different on the return journey in September, when the fields displayed glorious verdant-green rice shoots maturing and swaying in the breeze of a hot sunny day.

Living in the Issan region was harsh in 1945. Most families were very poor and survived on food found in the surrounding environment. A diet of ant eggs captured from nests high in the trees, together with wild mushrooms and new bamboo shoots, was supplemented with sticky rice and hen or duck eggs. Mangos, bananas, lemons, tamarinds, durian and papaya were freely available when in season. Homegrown chillies added intense heat to most dishes, with natural lemongrass and a plethora of spices creating intense flavours and a unique cuisine.

During the rainy season night-time excursions to catch frogs were a family occasion, and various flying bugs were a delicacy when roasted or fried. Fishing in rivers or ponds supplemented the diet and provided great entertainment, often ending in an improvised picnic. Cows and pigs were fattened up for the community to share, especially at a wedding or thanksgiving. Buffalos were working farm animals but, once their working life was over, they provided much-needed and welcome meat for the whole village.

Continuing on their journey to Ubon the men passed through the towns of Buriham, Surin and Sisaket. They were greeted at every station by curious locals and, if they were lucky, they caught a glimpse of the many Buddhist temples in each town.

Buddhism was very widely practised in the Issan region. Even in 1945 the temples displayed an opulence that far exceeded the collective poverty of a community. The temple was the centre of the village where everyone gathered not only to offer prayer and homage to Lord Buddha, but to socialise and support each other. Buddhist traditions and beliefs were passed down through the generations. It was not an intense religion but it encouraged respect and fairness as well as moral guidance.

Most males would at some time have been ordained as monk and lived in the temple for periods as short as a week or as long as a lifetime. They returned to the temple after a life-changing event, such as a family death, or if they had a vocational calling. Ordination is the ultimate display of respect and gratitude towards the family, especially to the mother, and is celebrated enthusiastically by the family and the village. From early morning prayers, alms giving and merit making, to blessings of homes and giving thanks for recovery from illness, the temple and the monks fulfilled a vital role in the village community.

The Prisoners eventually arrived at Ubon, or more precisely Warin Chamrap, or Varindra as it was also known in 1945. The railway line terminated about a mile before the river Mun. The land in between the station and the river was unstable and susceptible to serious flooding.

They were met by the curious eyes of locals and the close guard of the troops based in Ubon. Fergus Anckorn recalls arriving late at night and sleeping on the station platform before marching to the site designated for their camp. First, however, they had to cross the river Mun. The river Mun begins its journey close to Korat in the Khao Yai national park. After flowing through Ubon, it reaches the mighty river Mekong at the beautiful town of Khong Chiam about sixty miles further east, where the blue waters of the river Mun flow into the brown waters of the Mekong.

The town of Ubon was about a mile north from the station on the opposite bank of the river, and the only way to cross was by ferry. The logistics of ferrying the groups of men and their guards across the river took time.

A fleet of sampan narrow boats, seating four or five people one behind the other, was the main transport, but there was also a steam-powered ferry boat for large, bulky items.

The river Mun is wide, deep and fast flowing at Ubon and it required exceptional boating skills to control a boat, as well as steady nerves from its passengers.

Once across the river the men were in Ubon and were marched to the village of Ban Nong Phai some six miles to the north on the road to Mukdahan.

Chapter 8

UBON CAMP AND AIRSTRIP

On their march through Ubon the Prisoners passed government buildings, most of which were occupied by the Japanese. There was a terrace of police buildings, including the jailhouse, and a tree-lined recreation area that held regular weekend horse-racing events.

Shortly afterwards, they filed past the existing aerodrome. No doubt they wondered why another airstrip was required. Activity at the aerodrome was limited to surveillance and occasional supply flights. The landing surface was red laterite and reported to have good drainage, especially important in a monsoon area. However, aircraft belonging to the Royal Thai Air Force were in very short supply due to the scarcity of parts and fuel, and probably only one or two airworthy aircraft were stationed there. As for Japanese aircraft, there may have been some but most were stationed in the west where there was more demand. From here it was about a six-mile march north towards Mukdahan, which today is known as Highway 212.

The red laterite road lay before them like a long straight ribbon with only occasional small settlements on either side. In 1945 Khun Gim Jiarajinda was a young schoolgirl and she remembers Japanese soldiers touring the streets warning residents not to communicate with the Prisoners, otherwise they would be severely punished. The residents took heed of the warning and stood by the side of the road in silence watching the men with sympathetic curiosity.

As the Prisoners left the town, wild tangles of trees, scrub and bushes appeared on either side of the road. It could not be described as real jungle and was certainly nothing like the dense jungles in which they had survived along the railway.

Nevertheless, it seemed impenetrable and only occasionally punctuated with the odd field given over to growing rice or grazing for livestock.

The men marched in depressed silence alongside the equally dejected Japanese guards. After two hours, they arrived at the village of Ban Nong Phai. The guards called a halt at side of the road and pointed to some dry, empty fields a short distance from the road. The Prisoners had arrived at the Ubon camp.

The camp commander was called Major Chida. He was a diminutive figure in his mid-fifties and had been in command of most of the railway camps which the Prisoners had previously occupied. He announced that their priority was to construct the airstrip. Their morale sank further when they were told to sleep in the open and that the building of huts and other facilities could only take place when they were not working on the airstrip. This added to their ordeal because most of the men did not have blankets or sufficient clothing to withstand the relatively cold nights.

These bare desolate landscape in remote north-east Thailand intensified their depression and misery. They could be forgiven for feeling lost and forgotten. The Japanese guards probably had similar feelings; many of them had been away from home for long periods as well. Everyone's morale was deteriorating sharply, and no one was happy with the situation.

The airstrip site was located about one mile west of the camp. Work started by clearing trees and dense vegetation and constructing an access road at the northern end to connect with the main road. This road was only short but it was necessary to bring in stone ballast for the airstrip foundations. The Japanese enlisted local Thai families, including the youngest children, to quarry stone from fields near to the village of Ban Kao, three miles north from airstrip. Although the area was covered in forest and woodland, the stone was close to the surface and made an ideal foundation. With typical Thai ingenuity, the locals organised themselves into a production line. Several gangs of the strongest amongst them extracted the stone and loaded it into bamboo baskets, which were then placed onto wooden carts. The women and children drove the carts, pulled by buffalos, down the road to the airstrip.

Local resident Khun Thongdee Wongman remembers that, as a small boy, he and his family worked alongside other families each day transferring cartloads of stone to the airstrip construction site. In an interview in August 2018 he recalled that when they arrived at the airstrip the baskets were checked in by a Japanese soldier who paid fifteen baht for each one received. From this money the drivers retained five baht and gave the remaining ten baht to the quarrymen. The money was paid in special notes printed by the Japanese at their local office. They could spend the money locally and Thongdee recalls that once the war was over, the notes were exchanged for legal currency backed by the Thai government.

The savvier Thai villagers took advantage of the Japanese by placing false bottoms in the baskets thereby creating more loads and increasing their income. Ex-Ubon Prisoner Tom Brown remembers that the baskets were not always inspected thoroughly. It is possible that some of the inspectors could have been members of the Seri Thai resistance movement who had infiltrated the camp to gather intelligence. Soldaat Henk Gideonse, a Dutch Prisoner, refers in his memoir *Het Vergten Leger in de Jungle* to the 'Red Ant' in this type of role. At the very least devious antics took place, but the perpetrators were risked severe punishment if discovered.

It was not unusual for the locals to argue with each other when they shared the money. Occasionally serious fights would break out resulting in injury or, in at least one incident, death. Although there was a police force in Ubon, it was difficult to contact them because there was no telephone or radio communication. Many crimes were not reported as it took several days for the police to arrive and start an investigation. To provide some kind of justice and protection, minor crimes and disputes were mediated by the village leader who acted as judge and jury. If found guilty, the accused could be expelled from the village, resulting in loss of face for him and his family. This tradition still operates today, but only for the settlement of minor arguments. Nevertheless, the whole village hears about the dispute and judgement when the leader delivers his early morning announcements over the village tannoy system. But in the 1940's serious crimes such as suspected murder and assault were eventually dealt with by the police.

Work in the quarry and transporting the stone to the airstrip continued for almost three months. It was welcome extra income for the local village families. The quarried blocks of stone varied in size and were apparently similar to quartz, but easily broken up. Ex-Ubon Prisoner Maurice Naylor arrived at the camp in May 1945 and was immediately pressed into a stone-breaking gang. He then had to lay the stones into a foundation layer about two feet below the surface.

Meanwhile, there was the important matter of building a camp. The Prisoners built the usual style of hut out of bamboo posts and atap for the roof and walls. Finding pieces of bamboo of the right length and width was not always easy. Captain Harold Churchill was the senior doctor at Ubon and he recalls in his book *Prisoners on the Kwai* that the bamboo and atap were in short supply.

In an interview with elder residents from the village of Ban Nong Tokaeo (five miles from the camp), they recalled trading bamboo and other materials with the Japanese. They agreed to supply bamboo at a negotiated price of one baht for three pieces, and atap at one baht for four pieces. However, the demand was greater than the supply and further quantities had to be imported from elsewhere. Tom Brown recalls bamboo being floated down the river Mun to Ubon; he was in a gang tasked with transporting it back to the camp.

Thomas Whitehead was one of only four American POWs at Ubon. In an interview in February 1977 with Ronald Marcello at the North Texas State University of Oral History, he recalled that

Korean guards patrolled the camp until a high fence was erected and a moat around the camp was completed. (Remnants of the moat are still visible today.) Thomas recalled guards patrolling on the outside of the moat but does not recall any guards inside the camp compound. Tom Brown remembers local Thais stealing whatever they could find, but theft of fuel was most prevalent. On one occasion, copper telegraph wire was stripped off the poles between the camp and another Japanese outpost. Tom remembered with a wry smile that *just as soon as they finished putting it up, it disappeared the next night.'*

Dutch POW, Soldaat Henk Gideonse described how they constructed a hut in his memoirs *Het Vergten Leger in de Jungle.*

(Translated) The approximate dimensions of a hut were thirty metres by six metres. Bamboo poles were cut to various lengths but the longest ones, and the strongest, were three metres long and the poles for the sides were cut to two metres. These poles were then set into the ground about one metre apart. After firming up the poles, thinner poles were lashed to them using long thin strips of bamboo, which bound them into a solid structure. The atap roof was made out dried palm leaves which were draped over thin bamboo sticks lashed between the apex of the roof and the walls. This basic structure gave shelter more from the intense sun rather than the persistent rain.

Henk described weaving thin strips of bamboo into panels and attaching them to the shorter poles to make side walls. Finally, they constructed rudimentary bamboo sleeping platforms, which Henk called 'baleh-baleh'. Each hut accommodated up to one hundred men, possibly more, sleeping shoulder to shoulder. They did not have bedding, but bedbugs appeared everywhere.

The Prisoners' commanding officers were Regimental Sergeant-Major Sandy McTavish of the Argyll and Sutherland Highlanders, and Warrant Officer S. J. Slotboom of the Dutch Army. They were assisted by Major E. A. Smyth and Captain L. D. Stone, both of the Royal Army Medical Corps. At their previous camp in Nong Pladuk, most of the men had been under the command of the popular and fair-minded Colonel Phillip Toosey. RSM McTavish received the same respect at the Ubon camp.

The Japanese commanding officer was fifty-seven-year-old Major Chida Sotomatsu. He had held a command, mainly in Group 1, since the commencement of work on the Thailand-Burma railway in August 1942. He was known to many of the Prisoners. He was described as a man *'who was neither cruel or ruthless, but weak and incompetent'* and *'under the thumb'*. Like many elderly officers in the Imperial Japanese Army, he was controlled by his adjutants who were aggressive and domineering, and most of the time he did not really know what was going on around him. Discussions with Japanese camp commanders were always difficult and, given Major Chida's weak character, RSM McTavish's task was frustrating and difficult.

Despite the ever-present privations, the Prisoners' spirit could not be broken. RSM McTavish maintained strict discipline and kept morale intact with good management. As time passed, many Prisoners considered the camp less harsh than any of the previous camps in which they had been held. The Japanese and Korean guards were firm but, apart from the occasional incident, on the whole less aggressive. But it was still a miserable experience and everyone, Prisoners and guards, wished it would end.

Some of the men were allocated jobs within the camp, for example as medical staff and cooks. The majority worked on the airstrip, but some were marched back to Ubon (or if they were lucky were taken by truck) to work on the river Mun to ferry Japanese supplies and materials back and forth from the station.

Troops, stores and supplies were brought in from Bangkok by train. An OSS Sit Rep (A-55573) states that on the 9 May 1945 two trains arrived in Ubon carrying an estimated four hundred Japanese soldiers and seven carloads of supplies, chiefly gasoline, to be delivered to various Japanese locations throughout Ubon. A Japanese garrison was located one kilometre north of the railway station; several buildings on the north side of the river, for example Rajabhat university and the Roman Catholic church, had been commandeered for Japanese officers and administration.

Tom Brown remembers working on transportation and deliveries. On one occasion, with three other Prisoners, he was delivering bamboo to the camp in a dilapidated old truck. It was almost stripped of its body work but somehow managed to keep going. Upon arrival at the camp, the driver played a trick and jumped out of the cab leaving it in gear with the engine running. Tom had to clamber down quickly and stop it before it careered off and drew the attention of a guard.

Charles Steel, in his book *Burma Railway Man* (edited by Brian Best), refers to the main camp at Ban Nong Phai as Settitan. In addition to this camp, he mentions a smaller camp within the confines of the operational aerodrome in Ubon, which he calls Sensitai. The origin of these names is unknown, but there was a Japanese army unit called Hikojyo Setteitai (Airfield Construction Unit). Given that the Prisoners wrote down foreign words in phonetics, it is quite possible that spellings were not always correct or consistent. Other variations are 'Senitai' in an account from M. Soesman and 'Zenzietai' is found in another account by Lodewyk Jan Weygers.

The Sensitai camp held approximately four hundred men, mainly from the Dutch East Indies, accommodated in the relative luxury of existing brick-built huts. They were required to clear the land of scrub and bushes and work on building pillboxes and foxholes. These constructions were required to discourage robberies and defences from potential invading Allied forces. They also built fuel dumps and ammunition stores, but at other times they were called upon to assist in camp maintenance duties. Unfortunately, this work disturbed the habitats of giant red ants whose toxic sting constantly irritated the men. Henk Gideonse noted that he had heard that the formic acid of an ant sting was a good relief for rheumatism but he noted wryly that rheumatism was the only illness from which they did not suffer!

The guards at the Sensitai camp appeared to be more brutal. Dutch Prisoner M. Soesman tells of the poor treatment they received from the guards there, and Lieuntenant Cornelis B. Evers, in his book *Death Railway* states that the *'daily round of cursings and beatings by the guards was accepted as normal routine procedure'*. The men gave some of the guards' nicknames: 'the Gasoline King'; 'Goldtooth'; 'Bowleg'; 'Dracula'; 'Animal Abuser'; 'Ballpuller', and 'Mussolini'. The 'Oil King' was noted as being particularly brutal when he wielded his bamboo stick in a violent lunge followed by a vicious kick.

An intelligence report dated 20 June 1945 states that there were two companies of Japanese soldiers guarding the Ubon camp and that the main aerodrome at Ubon was being used as a training camp. It also reports that the camp was thought to be holding between 1,500 and 3,000 Prisoners who were American, Australian and Filipinos. Strangely, there was no mention of British Prisoners. The report states that there was a Prisoner of War camp in Korat where 150 men, either American or British, were being held to construct a road, but no further evidence has been found to support this. Finally, the report states that an estimated 200 French Prisoners were being held at Thakhek in French Indochina opposite Nakhon Phanom, north of Ubon. After the Japanese surrender, they were liberated and brought to Ubon.

Chapter 9

INSIDE THE UBON CAMP

One of the most important priorities was to construct a kitchen. The provision of food, whatever the quality, was vital. Warrant Officer II Charles Steel, of the 135 (Hertfordshire Yeomanry) Field Regiment Royal Artillery, was one of the first to arrive and held the responsibility of building the cookhouse and canteen facilities. It was his job to produce something – anything – out of nothing to keep the men's bodies and spirits together. Charles was allowed to travel under escort to Ubon's market, close to the river Mun ferry, to purchase supplies. He had high hopes that fresh fruit would be abundant, however, he was disappointed to find it was too expensive. Even eggs cost more than the budget allowed, although on some occasions he managed to buy a pig. He suspected that the Japanese were controlling the market and accumulating a healthy profit at his expense. Khun Thongdee Wongman recalls that Thai market stallholders probably refused to sell sub-standard produce to the Japanese if they knew it was for the Prisoners.

Unfortunately, by April not all the huts in the camp were complete and it was an ongoing task to build accommodation quickly enough for the stream of Prisoners arriving from Bangkok. Charles, however, was building the cookhouse and, in a letter to his wife, he was obviously pleased with the progress. For some reason at this time his shopping trips to Ubon market were curtailed and presumably he had to purchase locally or rely on what the Japanese provided. But by May the canteen and the cookhouse were finished to Charles' specifications. There was an office, counter space, a store and even sleeping quarters, but the centre piece was a home-made oven. The men had manufactured enough bricks from the abundant clay and sand on which the camp was built. The bricks varied in size, and presumably the smaller ones appeared towards the top of the oven. The largest bricks had a 'tongue and grove' moulded into them.

Corporal Roy Collins of the Royal Army Ordnance Corps recalls that the ovens were *'made of clay bricks with a hearth underneath. It didn't take long to make a meal after they were done with this'*. The oven was an instant success and raised morale at mealtimes, but this was short lived when the Japanese decided to take over the kitchen and facilities, leaving the Prisoners to build everything again elsewhere.

Sapper Whincup wrote that they made the bricks from clay soil within the camp to manufacture useful ovens, incinerators and de-lousing units. They dug a hole about six feet square and eighteen inches deep and filled it with clay and water. A group of men, nick named the *grape treaders of Ubon,* trampled the clay to make it malleable and another group made small wooden boxes to form the bricks. After a couple of days in the hot sun the bricks were ready for use.

Charles Steel was also responsible for the kitchen and canteen finances. In early June 1945, he had to face an interrogation from Japanese Lieutenant Oda when it was discovered that during April and May he had spent 20,000 dollars more than the amount of money given to him by the Japanese to buy food. The camp rules fixed the amount of money that Prisoners were allowed to have in their possession at any one time; any surplus cash was spent on food. In April and May the Japanese had bought food with the Prisoners' money. They passed the receipts to the administrator, who then compared the expenditure with the wages that had been paid.

Charles was called into Lieutenant Oda's office to account for the difference, and his explanation had to be good. As he approached the office he took deep breaths to keep calm and reminded himself not to hint at the truth, otherwise a witch-hunt would follow and every Prisoner in the camp would suffer.

Once in the office, Charles stood still with his hands behind his back. He explained that when the men were held in the previous camp at Nong Pladuk, they had saved money and brought it with them to Ubon. However, they could not spend their money in the first few weeks at Ubon because the canteen had limited stocks and was still under construction. The situation changed in April and May as the new canteen facilities opened resulting in an increase in sales revenue and a surplus of money.

Lieutenant Oda accepted Charles' unconvincing story. He probably knew where the surplus money really came from and let Charles off lightly. Charles had a good idea that the Japanese had stopped him from paying for the food at the market and taken over the purchasing themselves because they had started to rake off a profit at the Prisoners' expense. It seemed double dealing was taking place and, although everyone knew, the scam was being kept under wraps. Nevertheless, Charles was relieved that he had escaped with his improbable excuse.

But where *did* the extra money come from? The answer was that by now most of the prisoners were accomplished thieves of Japanese property and knew how to sell their spoils to the locals without the Japanese knowing. After three years in captivity, the Prisoners knew that the Thais would pay a good price for materials that were in short supply. Charles remembers that they sold nails to the locals for twenty cents each and a stick of solder could sell for twenty dollars.

Of equal importance was the availability of uncontaminated fresh water. Whilst working on the Thailand-Burma railway, Prisoners were exposed to the deadly waterborne diseases of cholera and dysentery. The river alongside the railway was severely contaminated by unsanitary conditions within the camps which could not be fully controlled. To make matters worse, the Romusha camps were completely disorganised and devoid of adequate hygiene and sanitation. Fatal outbreaks of cholera and dysentery inevitably spread quickly downstream to the other camps. Medical staff ordered river water to be boiled vigorously

67

several times before drinking or cooking. Despite these efforts, many Prisoners and even more Romusha civilians died.

There was no convenient river or stream near the Ubon camp, so the Japanese arranged delivery of water by tankers. This was expensive, and a continuous effort was required to keep a constant and adequate supply for the growing numbers of Prisoners who were arriving.

Dutch Prisoner Henk Gideonse recounts that working parties dug deep pits but failed to find an underground water source. He noted that Prisoners usually kept quiet about their skills, especially from the Japanese but a good water supply was essential to their survival. Having witnessed the fruitless efforts to find underground sources, a group of Dutch engineers stepped forward with a suggestion to construct a pump using various lengths and widths of bamboo to drill into the soil. The bamboo pumps were a great success and a good supply of fresh water, sufficient for washing, cooking and bathing, was soon available. The Japanese were so impressed that they sent plans of the process to other camps.

Great care was needed with the positioning of the latrines. There was no point in having a convenient supply of good water if it was going to be contaminated by raw sewage. Captain Eric Martin, who was the camp's dentist but also responsible for sanitation, decided to make latrines from forty-gallon oil drums. When full, the contents were emptied in an area away from the camp and local dwellings.

There is anecdotal evidence to suggest that the men billeted at the Ubon aerodrome camp bathed at the banks of the river Mun. This is quite possible as it was a relatively short walk from the aerodrome, and the quality of the river water at this point was satisfactory.

Because there was a good supply of uncontaminated water, the possibility of new outbreaks of waterborne diseases was considerably reduced. Nevertheless, the hospital was kept busy with a variety of illnesses. The Ubon medical diary reveals a great deal of useful information, though it does not include any references to Dutch personnel. The supposition is that the Dutch maintained their own hospital with their own medical staff, and any records made at the time have been lost.

There was a large contingent of medical staff sent to Ubon, all British except for one Australian private. Their priority was to attend to the British, Australian and Americans but presumably they would also help the Dutch if required. Records of Dutch medical staff at Ubon have not been found.

Medical staff sent to Ubon

Captains	*8*
Lieutenants	*1*
W.O. 1	*1*
W. O. 2	*2*
Staff Sergeants	*1*
Sergeants	*5*
Corporals	*9*
Lance Corporals	*5*
Privates	*61*
Total	*93*

The first entry in the medical diary appears on 25 February 1945. Although the criteria used by the Japanese to select Prisoners destined for Ubon is unknown, it is likely that many men who were fit and strong enough decided to volunteer. Numbers would be added from the ranks, but presumably the sick were left at Nong Pladuk hospital camp. Many of the men had contracted illnesses and infections in previous camps and hoped they would not recur at Ubon, not least because adequate medical supplies remained scarce.

The medical diary reveals an in-depth view of the health of the Ubon POWs. It is surprising, but nevertheless reassuring and comforting, that out of the 1,566 British, Australian and American Prisoners only 536 (34%) of them required medical treatment during their stay at Ubon. There was only one case of suspected cholera but the assumption is that this was either unfounded or treated successfully.

The most common diagnosis was recurring malaria symptoms (154 men presenting 194 cases) followed by dysentery (104 men presenting 122 cases). The analysis reveals that some men had recurring episodes or else a variation of a disease, or it accompanied another complaint, for example malaria with jaundice, or dysentery with hookworm.

The diary discloses two deaths. The first is the sad fate of Private Robert W. Merritt of the Australian Imperial Force, who was shot in the back by Japanese guards on 14 March 1945. (Details of this incident can be found in the next chapter.) The second entry records the death of Brigadier Hendrik Stadman of the Dutch East Indies Army on the 4 August 1945. His cause of death was pneumonia and it is stated that he 'died in Dutch Hospital', suggesting that the Dutch did in fact have separate facilities.

There were two further deaths, both of which are not recorded in the diary. Salomon Abas of the 5th Battalion Royal Dutch Army was shot on 26 April 1945 whilst trying to escape, and Sergeant Major Douwe Beers is known to have died from cholera on 26 April 1945. Anecdotal evidence from local village elders suggests that more deaths occurred but it is inconceivable to assume that the deaths of Prisoners would not have been officially recorded. Perhaps the locals witnessed Japanese deaths.

The most serious case involved amputation. A detailed analysis discloses 174 different presentations, and several unfortunate men appear to have had more than one complaint. The eldest patient was Private Flanigan, who was fifty-two years old, and there were four men whose ages are recorded as twenty-two years. The average age of all admissions was twenty-nine years and eleven months.

Private Green of the East Surreys was admitted six times with recurring bouts of malaria, and spent a total of forty-one nights in the hospital. The unfortunate Corporal Westlake, who was a medical orderly, appears to have stayed for a total of 132 continuous nights with *'Spore foot 7 jaundice'*. What this diagnosis represents is unclear.

There was a total of 706 admissions, which includes men admitted on more than one occasion, and 8,471 bed nights created between the first admission on 25 February and the last entry in the diary dated 31 August. There was a higher number of admissions due to malaria-related conditions during February and March whilst setting up the camp. In total, malarial presentations accounted for 1,060 bed nights, which is 12.5% of the total.

Although fewer Prisoners with dysentery-related conditions were admitted than those with malaria, they stayed in hospital much longer. A total of 2,213 bed nights were recorded, which is 26% of the total. There was a noticeable spike in July and during the week before liberation. Dysentery is very serious and can lead to death without proper treatment and care. The fact that there were no recorded deaths from the disease is testament to the skill of the medical staff, especially given that they would not have had adequate medication. In addition, a better quality water supply and improved sanitation management were significant factors in controlling infection. At the time of liberation, there were seventeen cases of dysentery in the hospital and the repatriation of these patients to Bangkok was a priority.

The Senior Medical Officer was Captain Harold Churchill, who qualified as a doctor in 1931 and practised in Norfolk. He joined the RAMC following the Dunkirk evacuation and worked in military hospitals in Scotland. His desire to see more action saw him attached to the Indian Army as Medical Officer. In January 1942 he transferred to Singapore with the Punjabi Brigade where he was captured. He was transferred to various camps along the railway where he succumbed to malaria and dysentery. Eventually he worked at the hospital camp of Nong Pladuk 2 where there were almost 5,000 sick men. His medical skills were required when Allied aircraft bombed that camp on 6 September

1944, leaving ninety-eight British and Dutch Prisoners dead and more than 200 wounded.

The camp dentist was Captain Eric Martin, also of the RAMC. In an interview he provided to the Imperial War Museum in May 2002, he gives an insight into how difficult it was to provide treatment for those with dental problems. Diet and lack of proper facilities to allow basic oral hygiene created many tooth issues. At a previous camp, he remembered asking a Prisoner called Addison to acquire a cocaine-based anaesthetic. Addison somehow obtained eight ounces of cocaine hydrochloride. It was a good anaesthetic – but care was needed to administer it correctly! They made an ingenious distillation apparatus to dilute the main ingredient to the correct strength. Captain Martin used this compound for the remainder of his captivity.

Captain Martin also tells of his train journey from Singapore to Ban Pong, during which he extracted a troublesome tooth from a fellow Prisoner. The train stopped at an unknown station where a large crowd had assembled under bright arc lights that illuminated the platform. The man with toothache was in agony and Captain Martin decided to treat him on the station platform in front of the crowd. His assistant held the man down whilst he was given an injection. The crowd fell silent as the Captain placed his forceps on the offending tooth. After three minutes of painful *'prolonged controlled force'*, he had to stop his attempt to extract the tooth because the soldier was in even greater pain. The crowd resumed talking and mulled around, hoping for further action. After a few minutes Captain Martin tried again. The crowd fell silent once more, transfixed by the performance in front of them. A minute later Captain Martin triumphantly held the monstrosity of a tooth aloft and the crowd burst into spontaneous applause. The tooth was thrown to a group of boys, who scrambled and jostled to claim ownership of it.

Interestingly, the medical diary stated the patient's given religion, which is summarised below.

Baptist   9

Church of England	*361*
Christian Scientist	*3*
Congregationalist	*7*
GC?	*1*
Jewish	*4*
Methodist	*21*
Non-Conformist	*1*
Presbyterian	*39*
Roman Catholic	*64*
Salvation Army	*2*
UB?	*1*
Unitarian	*1*
WB?	*1*
Wesleyan	*6*
Not stated	*22*
Total	*543*

The camp Chaplain was a Methodist minister called Padre Christopher Ross. A chapel was eventually constructed from the usual bamboo and atap and services were held in the evenings. Attendance was probably good, but Padre Ross had to compete against a choir of cicadas and croaking frogs.

Many men found their faith whilst facing adversity in the prison camps. Faith and companionship gave them hope that one day they would be with their families again. Of course, not all Prisoners had the same disposition, but for many the comforting words from a man of God were something to hold on to; whatever else they could do, the Japanese could not take that away from them.

Captain Churchill recollects that Padre Ross quoted from the Sermon on Mount, which is often admired as a *'summary of how Christians should live their lives'*. We may never know the precise content of Padre Ross's preaching, but Captain Churchill remembers him talking about the birds who *'sow not, neither reap nor gather into barns'* and *'to the lilies whose glory was greater than Solomon's'*. The passage most likely spoken by Padre Ross is from Matthew 6:25–34:

'Therefore, I say unto you. Take no thought for your life, what ye shall eat or what ye shall drink, nor yet for your body, what ye shall put on. Is not the life more than meat, and the body more than raiment? Behold the fowls of the air: for they sow not, neither do they reap, nor gather into barns; yet your heavenly Father feedeth them. Are ye not much better than they? Which of you by taking thought can add one cubit unto his stature? And why take ye thought for raiment? Consider the lilies of the field, how they grow; they toil not, neither do they spin.
And yet I say unto you, that even Solomon in all his glory was not arrayed like one of these. Wherefore, if God so clothe the grass of the field, which today is and tomorrow is cast into the oven, shall he not much more clothe you, O you of little faith? Therefore, take no thought saying, "What shall we eat?" or "What shall we drink?" or "Wherewithal shall be clothed?" (For after all these things do the Gentiles seek) for your heavenly Father knoweth that ye need have need of all these things. But seek ye first the kingdom of God, and his righteousness; and all these things shall be added unto you. Take therefore no thought for the morrow; for the morrow shall take thought for the things for itself. Sufficient unto the day is the evil thereof.'

These powerful words encouraged the most hardened Prisoners, giving them the hope they were looking for and comfort when their spirits were low. The version quoted above is taken from the Bible issued to all service personnel in September 1939, in which His Majesty King George VI wrote this message:

'For centuries the Bible has been a wholesome and strengthening influence in our national life, and it behoves us in these momentous days to turn with renewed faith to the Divine source of comfort and inspiration.'

Maurice Naylor recalls a particular prayer meeting on 5 August 1945 led by a senior NCO after a Sunday evening *tenko*. About ten Prisoners, whose faith was Roman Catholic, met in secret because they feared the Japanese would mistake them for an escape committee. They started a novena to the Blessed Virgin

Mary in preparation for the Feast of Assumption on 15 August. They then prayed on nine successive nights for an early and safe release. Their faith and beliefs were reward as their prayers were answered on the day the Japanese surrendered.

In addition to the church, there was great enthusiasm for the theatre. Amongst the men were several who were accomplished actors, musicians, singers, magicians and comedians. These creative and inspirational men did not need much encouragement to come forward to entertain their comrades. They certainly brought much needed cheer and merriment into the camp. In previous camps, especially after the railway was completed, organised entertainment was a popular distraction from the drudgery of monotonous labour and the boredom of captivity. For the entertainers, the production of variety shows, plays and concerts was an outlet to show off their talent for writing, producing and directing plays. But there were opportunities for anyone and everyone: costume makers; makeup artists; set designers, and lighting and artworkers.

By the time the men arrived in Ubon, the entertainers were well rehearsed and full of ideas about what they could accomplish. Their dedicated impresario, Private Bob Gale, provided inspiration and motivation. Throughout his imprisonment Private Gale produced many musicals and wrote more than forty songs. His enthusiasm and natural talent as an entertainer lifted spirits during the darkest hours. Before the war, he had formed a dance band at the age of sixteen and played in the dance halls of Kent's seaside resorts. He played the guitar and was spotted by Arthur Rosebery, who invited him to join his famous band at the Paradise Club in London. When the war broke out, Private Gale joined 137 Field Regiment and became conductor for their bands.

One of his many stories tells of an incident at the Hammersmith Palais where he was rehearsing for a microphone balance test. He recalls that, *'It is always a habit of mine to strum my guitar before playing but on this particular occasion Noel Coward was rehearsing a number. He sent one of the attendants to ask me to keep quiet.'*

To present a show, the men needed a theatre but the priority was building huts, kitchens and medical units. Camp Commandant Major Chida was under strict orders to complete the airstrip as quickly as possible, so he was not in a position, or mood, to allow the men any leisure time to rehearse and build sets for a production. However, the Prisoners made great progress with the airstrip construction and, by May 1945, Major Chida relented and allowed theatrical productions to begin.

At first, because there was no stage, impromptu performances were arranged in an open space. They were an instant and tremendous success amongst everyone in the camp. In one improvised show the comedians raised raucous laughter amongst the audience, and the onlooking Japanese guards mistakenly thought that the joke was directed at them. They immediately took retribution against the comedians and those seen to be laughing. This incident taught the men to suppress their giggles but on another occasion a parody included a marching officer, and the audience could not supress their sniggers. The Japanese thought another joke was being directed towards them. They grew angry and stopped the show, whereupon they started to beat the actor. At this point the whole audience erupted into raucous laughter in support of the hapless actor. Following this incident, Major Chida punished the men by banning further performances.

However, during the suspension Captain Martin sought Major Chida's approval to build a theatre. By this time the camp was settled and progress on the airstrip satisfied the Japanese Major. There was no shortage of volunteers to build it in their spare time. The men had formed an entertainment group and called themselves the '*Ubon Concert Party'*. With renewed confidence and enthusiasm, scripts were written for plays, revues and concerts. They designed and built sets, sewed costumes and painted artwork, including advertising posters. By 20 June the theatre was ready and the opening show, called *The Hollywood Revue,* was performed. The set consisted of a car parked between two walls. The door of the car opened and out stepped a performer impersonating a Hollywood movie star, very often a female movie star such as Mae West.

The site chosen for the theatre was adjacent to the parade ground. Earth had to be moved by hand to create a platform, which was about three feet high at the front rising to four feet at the back. This was designed so that the audience at the front could see the whole stage as well as the audience on the back rows. The building was made from bamboo, with woven bamboo matting and atap. Rice sacks were sewn together to make curtains and backdrops. There was a tree, which was hollowed out, next to the stage. Fergus Anckorn, the famous magician, recalls hiding *'illicit things'* in the tree and said that he would have hidden there himself if the Japanese had threatened execution.

The men working on the productions eagerly used their skills or learnt new ones. One such participant was Sergeant John Sartin, who was an explosives expert in the Royal Engineers. Sergeant Sartin was captured behind Japanese lines in Malaya whilst operating in the SOE under Colonel Freddie Spencer Chapman. In Ubon he was employed as a seamstress.

Those not involved in the shows made up the audience and thoroughly enjoyed great performances. The theatre was a great source of distraction. Once it had opened, there was a regular programme of performances.

In due course, it appeared that the shows might have been responsible for a thawing out of the frosty relationship between the Prisoners and the Japanese. Major Chida was fond of music and generally supported the men and their thespian spirit, providing they did not overstep the line, of course. In truth, he could not resist getting involved. The concert party had to humour him to stay out of trouble, but it was not easy.

On several occasions Major Chida insisted Harry 'Ace' Connolly, who led a band called the Kings of Swing, play at least fifteen minutes of his selected Japanese music. Ace was a fine musician, but his repertoire did not extend to Japanese music. Major Chida called him into his office and played some tunes on his flute. Ace then had to transcribe what he could remember, take this to a rapidly arranged band rehearsal and then play the unfamiliar tunes to a packed house of Prisoners, guards and Major Chida himself.

The climate in north-east Thailand was quite different to that along the railway and the river near Kanchanaburi.

Rainfall (inches)

Year	Kanchanaburi	Ubon
1942	103.0	158.3
1943	114.1	185.9
1944	Not available	140.1
1945	89.1	186.6
Mean 1911-1960	100.0	149.4

The readings above show that the annual rainfall between 1942 and 1945 in Kanchanaburi, which was the nearest location to the jungles of the west, was consistently less than the rainfall at Ubon for the same period. Comparisons are not available for other weather conditions between the two areas, and it is quite possible that further along the railway the rainfall was higher than in Kanchanaburi.

The men started to arrive in Ubon from late February through to early May. At that time of year, they would have experienced daytime temperatures exceeding 32°C. This was the dry season, and clear skies would have resulted in night-time temperatures falling to 23°C, which would have felt relatively cool after such a hot day. From early May the temperatures started to fall slightly as the wet season gradually made its presence felt. With the increase in rainfall there was a corresponding increase in humidity as the monsoon arrived. The rainfall reached a peak in early September. From mid-October, on average, rainfall decreased rapidly as the dry season took over again. Daytime temperatures remained relatively cool throughout this period at an average of 26°C. Anecdotal accounts refer to the monsoon rains in 1945 being heavy and the river Mun flooding to over a mile in width at some points.

This area of north-east Thailand is monotonously flat and susceptible to flooding over a wide area. The landscape around the Ubon camp was mainly trees and shrub land, with occasional rice fields. The Thailand-Burma railway, to the west of Kanchanaburi, soon reached dense jungle on steep hillsides alongside the river. The two areas were very different to each other.

Several POWs took an interest in the nature and wildlife around the Ubon camp. Captain Harold Churchill noted that there was a migration of birds to the rivers and marshes. He was obviously a keen ornithologist and made sightings of larks, pipets, flycatchers, orioles and hoopoes; he had a particular fondness for the ioras and its constant birdsong.

One day William Wilder found a stick insect that he recalls being almost seventeen inches long. In addition, he noted butterflies, scorpions, ants, beetles, snakes and huge centipedes. Hugh King Ashby writes about frequently observing flying lizards at nightfall. A scavenger bird identified as a Turkey Buzzard caught the eye of Charles Steel, who witnessed gangs of them picking through the rubbish.

The men had to tolerate many different kinds of ants. These went into every nook and cranny, but it was the vicious red ant and its stinging bite that caused the greatest discomfort, particularly when they were trying to sleep on open ground. Hugh King Ashby remembers watching working ants trailing up and down a tree. Lying in wait, disguised by the bark, was another insect he called the 'lancer' waiting patiently for an over-inquisitive ant. The sweet-smelling saliva from the lancer invited the ant to stray from its path. When it was within striking distance, the lancer stabbed the hapless ant, and then appeared to suck at its body until everything was extracted, at which point it discarded the shell-like remains with a nonchalant flick of its neck.

Other irritating insect pests included the centipede (Scolopendra subspinipes and its cousins). These insects can grow up to twenty centimetres and its bite, although not poisonous, is particularly vicious and painful. Charles Steel was bitten on his arm, which swelled and gave him the same effects as a bout of malaria. There were spiders of all shapes and sizes, including the tarantula (Thai Zebra and Cobalt Blue). These nasty creatures live underground or in decayed tree bark behind a thick silk defence. Spiders' webs stretched for several metres between trees and anyone not paying attention whilst walking could easily become entangled with transparent silky fibres. The men also had to contend with scorpions.

Thailand is a habitat for many of the world's most beautiful butterflies and moths, and many references to these can be found in the Prisoners' writings and diaries. There are hundreds of species of birds and at dusk the men witnessed scores of bats flying out of their roosts for their evening banquet of bugs and flies. Snakes were very common, and some were dangerous. Tree snakes, pythons, cobras and water snakes were just a few that the Prisoners encountered almost anywhere in the camp or when they were at work on the airfield. More common were geckoes and lizards patiently waiting to catch their insect prey.

There were probably monkeys living in the trees around the Ubon camp, and badgers, mongoose, martens and mice would be close by.

Less pleasant was the constant swarm of flies. Sick Prisoners were ordered to occupy their time by catching them. Each day they had to fill a small bottle of the repugnant insects for which they received a small payment. A Prisoner under the watchful eye of a guard took the flies to the incinerator to be destroyed. But Sapper Whincup, who was in charge of the incinerator, put a flat sheet of metal just below the top of the incinerator to prevent the flies from falling into the furnace and being destroyed. The guards were unaware of this and when they left he removed the sheet, recovered the flies, re-filled the bottles and secretly returned them to the sick Prisoners ready for the next day.

Brilliant sunsets of reds, oranges, pinks and purples, accompanied by the deafening cry of cicadas, brought each hot day to a close. Darkness fell quickly and the night air became cacophonous with the constant croaking of thousands of frogs in the trees and rice fields, especially if it was raining and humid. As the night progressed, insects and bugs of all shapes and sizes were attracted by the light and were irritating to anyone who happened to be in their path. The only respite for the Prisoners was the cover of a blanket, if they had one.

Several Prisoners recalled that, in general, day-to-day living in the Ubon camp was better than they had experienced in previous camps along the railway. Although the Japanese still maintained a strict regime, they were less ruthless. Falling out of line still brought serious consequences for the men but, perhaps because the camp was a long way from the camps in the west, it allowed the Japanese to be slightly more relaxed.

The men worked hard to construct the airstrip despite having to accept the varying quality of food and medical care. On a personal level, each man brought with him the mental strain and scars of captivity from the previous three years. Understandably, it was difficult to endure each day and night in circumstances in which they were isolated from the rest of the world. They could only live from day to day and hope their captivity would end as soon as possible. Personal diaries and interviews have provided a brief insight of the camp's daily life and, in some cases, revealed the Prisoners' inner thoughts and the strains of imprisonment.

Companionship was vitally important to keep up morale and spirits. Many of the men owed their survival to the friendship of their mates. They relied on each other to see them through to the next day. Inevitably, given the stresses and strains they were under, controlling mental pressure in such harsh conditions was difficult.

Before the Prisoners were sent to Ubon the Japanese separated the men from their officers in an attempt to break their solidarity and create disorder within the ranks. This tactic failed, but inevitably there were flashpoints between individuals, nationalities and rank, as well as fall-outs between medical, catering and security services.

One such incident at Ubon was recorded by Charles Steel. It occurred between his kitchen staff and the commissioned medical officers. At one particular mealtime, a medical officer pushed his way to the front of a queue of work-weary Prisoners who were waiting patiently for their meal. The canteen manager refused him the preferential treatment he demanded. The ensuing argument exposed further irritations that had been simmering for some time. The hut Warrant Officers complained that the medical orderlies were consistently late for sick parades and continually demanded preferential treatment. Both sides were threatened with a court martial but, despite the warning, the kitchen staff continued to disregard their *'I am an officer'* attitude. Throughout his diary, Charles criticises the officers with observations that they *'spend time on their backs'* or they jibed the regular soldiers. In another example, a particular grudge festered and resulted in a revenge attack in which a Prisoner found scorpions in his bedding.

By the time they arrived in Ubon, most of the men had lost many, if not all, of their personal and basic possessions. Their clothes had worn out and they were forced to wear rudimentary loincloths commonly referred to as a *'jap happy'*. This nappy-like garment protected them from the embarrassment of nudity but did little else. Footwear was almost non-existent, except for the lucky few who owned a type of clog or wooden sandal crudely improvised out of bamboo. Valuable personal and sentimental possessions had mostly been confiscated (stolen) by the Japanese well before they arrived in Ubon, or traded with local villagers in exchange for additional food or medicine.

The Japanese had opportunities to improve the comfort of the Prisoners but they chose to do nothing. After the war ended, it transpired that under Major Chida's orders the Japanese purposely withheld hundreds of Red Cross parcels, frequently stealing items from them for their own use. As a result, many Prisoners suffered needlessly. Clothing, blankets and medicine were withheld, causing hardship and prolonging illness. To their absolute shame, scores of parcels were found in a storeroom at Ubon after the Japanese surrendered. Anecdotally it appears many Japanese officers did very little to help even their own other ranks, especially the Koreans, with uniforms or the provision of satisfactory bedding.

The Japanese continued to carry out regular hut searches with the threat of severe punishment hanging over the Prisoners if disallowed items were discovered. This did nothing to calm the already high stress levels. Unfortunately there was petty thieving amongst the Prisoners, which was unpleasant and upsetting for the victims.

Sometimes an unexpected event would instantly raise spirits. Obviously camp entertainment was a pleasant distraction, but even insignificant incidents helped to improve the mood. For example, William Wilder writes of a snake in his Ubon hut that slunk its way into the roof followed by the hilarious antics attempting to catch it.

Surprisingly, the Japanese allowed the men to keep pets in the camp. There was a bull-terrier bitch called Peggy, who was first befriended by a group of Prisoners at Singapore. Charles Steel saw her again at Tamarkan, where apparently she gave birth to two puppies, one called Speedo and the other Resto. Sadly, Peggy was cruelly bayoneted by a Japanese guard, but she was nursed back to health and travelled to Ubon. One day, Peggy introduced her new boyfriend to the assembled Prisoners on the Ubon parade ground. Without any hint of embarrassment or shame, the amorous couple shared a moment of passion with the entire parade. A few months later, eight puppies were running around the camp. Peggy was at home with the Prisoners but growled and barked fiercely at the Japanese. A comical account of Peggy's encounter was recorded in the camp's post liberation newsletter which was called *Newsphere*:

Interview with a Lady…
'Good afternoon Peggy,' I said. 'I wonder if you could say a few words to our readers on the famous Ubon octet you have recently produced?'
Peggy simpered and blushed, 'There is not much I can say to a crowd of men is there?'
'I don't know about that' I replied, 'you were not so reticent about your courtship.'
'I don't see the need for vulgarity,' said Peggy.
'No vulgarity intended,' I responded. 'It's just your point of view.'
'If you are coming to that' said Peggy, 'my point of view for the last three and a half years has been a continual procession of half or completely naked POWs. Hardly helps a girl's moral tone, does it?'
'I suppose the pups will be brought up to call Jimmy "father", won't they?'
'Yes, I suppose so,' said Peggy without enthusiasm.
'Your name has been connected with that of a large shaggy black and white IJA animal. In view of the fact that some of the pups have black markings, perhaps you would care to make a statement?'
'As a matter of fact, I deny everything' said Peggy, 'but he is a nice gentlemanly dog, and a girl likes to do her friends a favour now and again.'

Charles also noted that two 'tame' monkeys roamed around the Ubon camp. One was killed by a Korean guard and shortly after the surviving monkey was smuggled out of the camp for its safety. Also, at Ubon there were plenty of stray chickens, including one called Nelson because it only had one eye.

After three years of confinement and hard labour, every Prisoner arriving at Ubon was tired and depressed. They had suffered enough, and memories of the recent disastrous friendly-fire

Allied bombings at Nong Pladuk and Bangkok made them wonder if they would ever get out alive. They did not realise that, because Ubon was located in the far north-east of Thailand, Allied aircraft could not make the return journey from their bases in India and Ceylon fully laden with heavy bombs. In any case, there were more strategic targets in the west, particularly in Bangkok and along the railway. Consequently, after several weeks without an air raid, the Prisoners began to feel safer; though they remained vigilant, at least there was one less threat to their lives.

There are no medical records of depression or suicide attempts at Ubon, but comments made by some Prisoners reflect the air of despondency and low spirits. William Wilder writes of his anxiety about moving from Nong Pladuk to Ubon. He hated moving and wanted to arrive at Ubon as soon as possible but the long, slow journey did not lift his black mood. Just after he arrived, he wrote in his diary that he was '*in a bad way*'. He let his thoughts drift into imagining a homecoming '*if it will ever come*' and admitting that he was '*sick of this existence*' and '*when will it all end*'. Maurice Naylor often wondered, especially at night time, how they would get out of their situation alive.

In their quiet moments, especially during the dead of night, Prisoners' thoughts turned to wives, girlfriends and family. Private Len Knott, a medical orderly, in a note to his then-girlfriend Joan, tells her of '*the tortured nights of thinking about you, remembering things which only made sleep more difficult*'. (Happily, when Len eventually arrived home, he and Joan were married.) Some men harboured even worse fears. After three and a half years without contact, it was a distinct possibility that their wives or girlfriends might have assumed their husbands or boyfriends had been killed and chosen to marry someone else and start to raise a family. Sadly, this did happen all too often. Other nightly fears led to thoughts of Japanese reaction to defeat and, in particular, if they would retaliate with violence or a threat of death.

Soldaat Henk Gideonse made an interesting and thought-provoking observation. He considered that many Prisoners lost sight of who they were actually working for because they became so absorbed in their work. He believed that a Prisoner had to think negatively in order to be positive: '*how can I achieve as little as possible with as little effort as possible in as long a time as possible?*' Henk believed that the Japanese were indoctrinated with a work ethic; he advised that because of this as long as a Prisoner looked busy, preferably doing nothing, the guards would leave him alone and he would avoid punishment. This may have been true at Ubon, but it was a different story when the men worked on the railway.

However, on the whole it is believed that the Japanese guards at Ubon treated their Prisoners reasonably well. Maurice Naylor recalls that working on the airstrip '*was not unduly arduous and the Japanese supervisors were reasonable. There was no speedo or sense of urgency as had been the case on the Thailand-Burma railway in 1943.*' He continued '*looking back it was probably my best period in captivity.*'

Thomas Brown and Harold Pleasance also remember the Ubon camp being less severe than previous camps. It is recorded that on several occasions whilst marching to the Settitan airstrip, a Japanese guard would hand his rifle to a Prisoner to carry and look after whilst he rolled a cigarette and smoked it.

However, not all Prisoners agree that their treatment at Ubon was less intense. Dutch Prisoner Lodewyk Jan Weygers writes of brutal beatings and poor treatment from the Japanese guards at the Sensitai camp at Ubon aerodrome. A speculative reason for this type of treatment is that the Sensitai camp was some distance from the main Ubon camp and was probably commanded by Japanese junior officers who thought they could act with impunity. In an interview with village elders from Ban Nong Tokaeo they remember that if a Thai person (and possibly a Prisoner) was caught stealing or even suspected of theft, they would be placed in a rice sack. The guards then poured scores of vicious red ants into the bag and tied it up. The unfortunate victim was bitten and irritated to the point of delirium.

Major Chida issued orders that were especially irksome to the Prisoners. One common demand was that every Prisoner must have a shaved head. The reasoning behind this is not clear, neither is it certain how this was achieved. Presumably shaving blades were too blunt to shave beards, let alone heads, and there were 3,000 heads to keep hairless.

Discussion groups were popular in most camps and it is safe to assume that they were continued at Ubon. Many Prisoners enjoyed a cigarette, but they were in short supply. However, at Ubon there was a dubious supply of different grades of 'Thai weed'. Any available paper was used to roll a primitive cigarette but, for some at least, it was something to smoke and a brief respite from the stress and strain. It was also fairly common for Prisoners working on the airstrip to buy or barter for cigarettes from enterprising local Thai people who regularly sat and watched the men working.

Gunner James Cowan of the Australian Army Eighth Division noted that the men often played cricket or football with improvised equipment when they were allowed a rest day. By granting this privilege, Major Chida appears to have been more relaxed than he was in the railway camps. As the men participated in organised recreation, they must have been in reasonable physical shape.

Thoughts of an end to the war and going home were never far away. The war in Europe ended in May 1945. It was a time of important news, and the local Thai villagers were eager to pass it on, but the language barrier made it difficult to communicate properly. Nevertheless, whatever the news was, the reactions and body language of the Thais convinced the men that it must be good. It gave them reason to be optimistic. Before long, as they received news through their own channels, the Japanese realised that defeat was not far away. Consequently there was a change in their behaviour towards the Prisoners, although it was uncertain in which direction it was going.

Whatever mood Major Chida was in, he had to obey orders from his higher command. He was told to instruct the Prisoners to dig trenches ten feet wide and six feet deep across the airstrip. The Prisoners thought this was to prevent Allied aircraft from landing but, in fact, they had dug their own graves. Major Chida received further orders to execute all Prisoners in the event of an Allied invasion of Thailand. This was a common order sent to all Prisoner of War camps in the country.

Dutch Prisoner Lieutenant Cornelis B. Evers recorded that they were allowed to dig a swimming pool. It was a puzzling concession but they set to work with enthusiasm, even though they questioned the location because there was no local source of water to fill the pool. They later discovered that it was to be put to the same use as the trenches across the airstrip.

Chapter 10

ESCAPE AND DEATH

Escape attempts at Ubon were rare, but one evening in March 1945 Private Robert Merritt (TX5341) left the camp in an alleged effort to escape.

Robert was born in Derby, Tasmania on 11 November 1919. His army records show that he had worked as a copper miner but was unemployed when he enlisted into the 2/2 Pioneer Battalion on 29 April 1941. In his first year as a soldier his conduct often got him into trouble for minor disciplinary offences. On 2 November 1941 he embarked on the SS *Orcades* and left Sydney for service in the Middle East. He arrived on 24 November but soon found himself back on the SS *Orcades* on 31 January 1942, sailing to an unknown destination.

On 18 February, the ship arrived in Batavia where Robert and his unit fought Japanese paratroopers who had taken the island's oil fields and airstrips. They resisted the Japanese offensive until the 9 March, when they were ordered to ceasefire and Robert became a Prisoner of the Japanese. It is very likely that he was taken to the Bicycle Camp and transferred from there to Singapore.

From Singapore he was subsequently transferred to Thailand with Dunlop Force to work on the railway. He survived the privations of the railway and was eventually transferred to Ubon in February 1945 with a party of one hundred of his fellow countrymen.

On the evening of 14 March 1945, Robert left the camp. At roll call the following morning the Japanese discovered he was missing. However, a few hours later he returned to camp. Although he accounted for his whereabouts by showing the

Japanese officers where he had been, he did not satisfy them and they shot him dead.

Some eyewitness statements appear in Prisoners' diaries. The consensus is that Robert did indeed leave the camp sometime in the evening of 14 March. The reason for his leaving is uncertain; possibly he was meeting a contact to gather news or medical supplies and extra food. All accounts indicate that he returned the next morning, only to find that the Japanese were aware of his absence. He then apparently reported to the guard room. Later in the day, two guards and First Lieutenant Hosoda ordered him to show them his escape route and took him out of the camp. Shortly afterwards two shots were heard by men inside the camp.

Robert's body was brought back and taken to the hospital unit by unknown Prisoners. A post-mortem was carried out and the entry in the medical diary states that his cause of death was '*G.W.S. (gunshot wound) penetrating right scapula to right clavicle. Shot by I.J.A. whilst escaping.*' In other words, he was shot in the back in cold blood.

There was no inquiry or trial at Ubon in 1945, but in 2015 Robert's case was put to a tribunal convened to consider the 'Recognition for Far East Prisoners of War who were killed while escaping or following recapture.' It was concluded that there was a discrepancy between the reports taken from the Japanese records immediately after the war and Prisoner eyewitness statements.

The Japanese report on Robert's escape read: *'According to the monthly report for April 1945 from Thai camp, Merritt escaped on 14 March 1945 from Branch No 1 camp, located 9km north of UBON. When subsequently discovered in the jungle Merritt resisted arrest, whereupon 1st Lieutenant HOSODA gave orders to the search party to shoot. Two shots were fired, one of which killed Merritt instantly.'*

His tribunal case was unfortunately rejected, and he did not receive a posthumous award. Robert was buried at Ubon but, after the war ended, he was re-buried at Kanchanaburi War Cemetery.

There are no further entries in the British medical diary indicating deaths amongst the British, Australians or Americans. However, there is an entry stating that Brigadier Hendrik Stadman of the Netherlands East Indies Army died on 4 August 1945 in the Dutch hospital from pneumonia. He was re-buried at Kanchanaburi War Cemetery.

Sergeant Major Douwe Beers' record appears in the Dutch National Archives. It is documented that he died at Ubon 26 April 1945 from cholera. The record shows he was buried at a cemetery in Ubon, but this most probably is a reference to the Ubon camp. He was re-buried at Kanchanaburi War Cemetery.

Another Dutch soldier, Soldaat Salomon Abas, has two records in the Dutch National Archives. Both records state that he also died on 26 April 1945. One record is vague about place names, but the second record states he died at 19:00 on 26 April 1945 at a place '*4 km east of Ubon city, Ubon prefecture, Thailand.*' He died from a '*bullet wound on* [sic] *head, unnatural death.*' A further note states '*killed in accident.*' He was originally buried in Ubon, but was re-buried at Kanchanaburi War Cemetery, where his date of death is recorded as 24 April 1945.

Saloman was one of fourteen children and there is a very sad and shocking footnote relating to the fate of his family back in Europe. Saloman's father, Mozes, a Jewish merchant and diamond cutter, died at Mauthausen concentration camp in Upper Austria on 24 June 1942. His mother, Alida Morpurgo, died one year later on 2 July 1943 in Sobibor extermination camp in Poland. Of Salomon's fourteen siblings, three died at a young age before the start of the war and eight were murdered in Nazi concentration camps (five on the same day at Auschwitz). There was only one survivor, Joseph, and he lived to eighty-three years of age. The fate of the other sibling is not known.

Mauthausen and its subcamps were Nazi slave labour camps where an estimated 122,000 to 320,000 people of various ethnic origins were executed. At least a further 167,000 were sent to their deaths at Sobibor, which is regarded as the fourth deadliest German extermination camp after Belzec, Treblinka and Auschwitz. This is a stark reminder of the pain and suffering some families had to bear at the hands of the Allies' enemies.

There are a further three entries in the British medical diary for Ubon that record deaths but the dates suggest that the deaths probably occurred on the journey to Ubon. Private J. P. Dolan of the RASC died on 16 January 1945 from the effects of malaria. Lance Corporal Heath of the East Surreys died on 5 February 1945 from the effects of cholera. Soldaat Herman Bernard Lammers of the Netherlands East Indies Army died on 9 November 1944 from cerebral malaria. All three men are buried at Chungkai War Cemetery.

Chapter 11

JAPANESE LOCATIONS IN UBON

As well as the troops guarding the Prisoners, there were many more stationed in Ubon although the numbers frequently varied. They were located in various places throughout the town. An intelligence report from early May 1945 revealed approximately 400 Japanese troops and seven carloads of supplies arriving in Ubon by train from Bangkok.

It stated that there was a radio station and an arsenal located in a *'dark forest three miles north of Ubon between the Ubon – Yasothon road the Ubon–Mukdahan road, approximately one thousand yards from the Ubon–Mukdahan road'*.

Another report recorded that the Japanese army had about twenty-five trucks and there was a new army barracks located one kilometre north of Warin Chamrap railway station, south of the river and west of the road consisting of twelve *bashas*, (bamboo houses built on stilts to protect against monsoon floods).

There were no more than fourteen Japanese twin-engine light bombers at Ubon aerodrome. Other planes were flying two or three times per day with supplies of rice to Pakse in French Indochina, about eighty miles to the east, whilst several trucks carried weapons and machine tools for an air training centre they intended to establish there.

Most of the Japanese aircraft were located away from Ubon in positions where they would be more useful in responding to Allied attacks. At this stage, Ubon was not in range of Allied bomber aircraft. However, a report on the strength of the Royal

Thai Air Force dated 3 June 1945 informs that there were *'much supplies and some aircraft'* at Ubon. A shuttle service existed between Ubon and Udon Thani, which was *'a camouflaging movement using bombers'*. No further detail was submitted.

The Japanese commandeered several buildings in Ubon, including the Rajabhat university on the road now called Thanon Chayangkun and offices at Phra Kuman Roman Catholic school close to the centre of the town.

Several petrol dumps, a tank repair shop and explosive stores were constructed in the local area and at the aerodrome.

The railway station was located at Warin Chamrap, south of the river. Early maps display a loop branch line extending to the river and continuing onto the main line.

An intelligence report indicates that this line was situated at Bung Wei and led to *'a quarry with a telephone line'*.

The line has disappeared but there is evidence on the ground of its existence and a quarry is still in production.

In fact, the line terminated at what was once a rice mill and did not continue to the main line.

Kun Preecha Petin was a young boy living in the area just after the end of the war. His grandfather owned a large rice mill by the river. In an interview, he remembered that many people brought their rice to the mill to sell or de-husk for their own use.

The railway line was built especially for the mill to transport rice to the Bangkok markets.

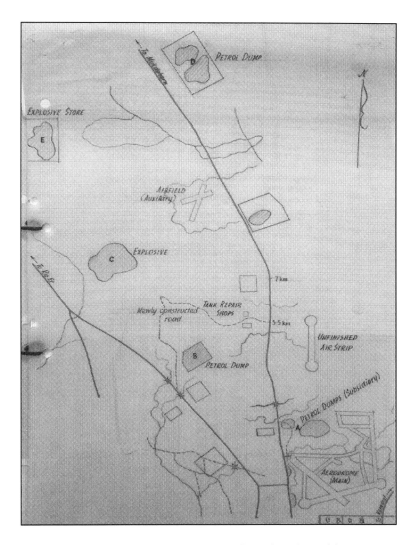

This sketch map above (Courtesy of National Archives Kew) was redrawn by British Intelligence from a rough drawing probably provided originally by a Seri Thai agent. It places the positions of Japanese assets in the Ubon area.

The airstrip under construction by the Prisoners and their camp are identified by *'Airfield (Auxillary)'* and the square shape on the opposite side of the red line, which today is Highway 212.

Further north on Highway 212 is the site of the quarry where stone was extracted for the foundations of the airstrip. It is possible that this is also the site of the petrol dump marked D on the sketch map.

West from the quarry is an explosive store, marked E. Evidence for this was provided by two elderly residents from the village of Ban Nong Tokaeo. They recall that Japanese troops excavated several bunkers in an area close to the village in which they intended to store arms and ammunition. The bunkers were excavated in the forest away from houses and the road. At least one bunker still remains, although today it amounts to no more than a large mound of earth. The residents remembered that the war ended before the bunkers were put to use.

The site marked 'Unfinished Airstrip' on the sketch map has not been located and there are no further records providing any evidence of this location. Neither is there any anecdotal evidence to suggest an additional airstrip was under construction at or close to that location.

The petrol dump marked B on the sketch map has not been located, but it is suggested that it may be in the vicinity of the newly opened Ubon zoo. Verification is needed. However, at Triam Udom Suksa Pattanakarn Ubon Ratchathani School, which is in the proximity of the zoo, there are buildings and ammunition storage units used by the United States Air Force during the Vietnam war when they were based at Ubon aerodrome in the 1960s.

The intelligence report attached to the above map details a plan of work to be carried out between 10 March 1945 and 20 June 1945. The Prisoners from the camp were presumably ordered to carry out this work. They were to establish a petrol dump at the north end of the aerodrome consisting of fifteen emplacements, each taking twenty drums of fuel at the point marked A on the sketch map. In addition, they were to establish emplacements for explosives and fifty drums of petrol at the site marked B, which the report states were four kilometres north-west of the aerodrome. At location C they were to construct fifty emplacements to store fifty bombs and ten emplacements for fuses and explosives. At locations D and E, they were to construct fifty emplacements each for fifty drums of petrol. Finally, the men were to construct small emplacements for petrol and explosives next to each runway to take up to twenty drums each.

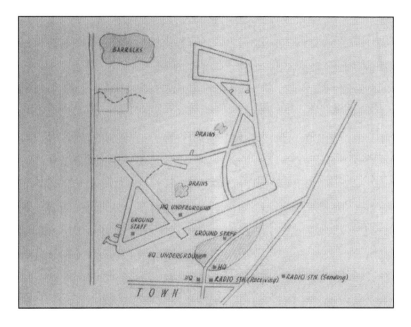

Also included in the intelligence report is a further sketch map (above, Courtesy of National Archives Kew) with a detailed *Plan of Construction of UBON South Aerodrome*. This plan is not the airstrip under construction by the Prisoners at Ban Nong Phai, but the aerodrome marked Aerodrome (Main) on the previous sketch. It is located in the centre of Ubon. In the intelligence report attached to the sketch it is identified as Pratum, the name of the locality in which today's aerodrome is situated. The length of the main runway is stated as 1,670 metres long by 100 metres wide and is described as all-weather, possibly laterite. It shows a secondary runway of some 1,000 metres long and 50 metres wide with a possible 1% slope. The taxiways total 6,404 metres in length and 30 metres wide. The intelligence report identifies drains and bridges and noted that there were fifteen large planes and fifteen small planes located under coconut plantations, probably camouflaged, around the airfield. Japanese air force Unit 9645 (GNI) occupied the aerodrome (as at April 1945). They had 5,000 drums each containing 200 litres of petrol, also 5,000 bombs and fuses and 200 auxilliary tanks for the planes. The Japanese were concerned to establish these stocks to keep the unit in continuous operation in the belief that Allied bombing raids were possible.

Another report entitled *Train Schedules and Movement of Troops and Supplies* dated 3 to 11 July 1945 stated that the following equipment was moved from Bangkok to Ubon:

550 rifles
8 trucks
12 generators
5 engines (type unknown)
About 300 oxygen cylinders
50 boxes incendiary bombs
155 boxes of ammunition
18 plane engines
2 plane wings
1 fuel truck
100 machine rigs
300 small bombs
2,000 pieces of road construction equipment
1,000 pairs of wooden shoes
100 drums of gasoline
6,150 wooden boxes of various sizes
4,000 bundles of paper wrapped objects

Ubon was not the only city in north-east Thailand to be occupied by the Japanese. Evidence shows that Japanese units were present in varying numbers in Sakhon Nakhon, Udon Thani, Mukdahan, Yasothon, Nakhon Phanom, Nong Khai, Mahasarakham and Khon Kaen. It is also known that small garrisons were located in small villages: for example, a unit of fifteen Japanese soldiers was stationed at Phibun Mangasahan, about forty miles east of Ubon. Their purpose is not known, but it was probably to keep the peace and gather intelligence. In an interview with Khun Nikom from Phibun Mangasahan, he showed where the Japanese made their camp, which was only 150 metres away from the local Seri Thai secret meeting place!

Chapter 12

THEY WERE THERE

Every single one of the 3,041 men who were kept captive at Ubon had a unique story of how they became a Prisoner of War. They gave up promising careers and futures to fight for their country. It isn't possible to collect the story of every Prisoner, but here are some impressive accounts.

Sergeant John Sartin MC – British Army
Sergeant John Sartin was a Royal Engineers demolition instructor attached to Special Operations Executive (SOE) 101STS (Special Training School) in Singapore. In December 1941, John was training Malayan resistance workers in techniques of sabotage and guerrilla tactics so that they would know how to disrupt Japanese lines. One of the principal instructors at 101STS was Colonel Freddie Spencer Chapman. On 19 December 1941 he selected John to join him in an operation in Malaya with orders to *'organise and lead reconnaissance and operational parties behind Japanese enemy lines'*.

By the beginning of February 1942, they had established camp in the jungle near to Tanjong Malim, forty miles north of Kuala Lumpur. Each night for two weeks they left their camp, fully armed with heavy backpacks of explosives, to go to selected targets on the Singapore to Thailand railway line. Their objective was to interrupt the Japanese supply lines that supported their advancing troops who were heading towards Singapore. They were so successful that Sergeant Sartin was awarded the Military Cross. His citation describes his brave action:

(Sergeant) Sartin displayed considerable skill (as a demolition expert), courage and resolution, operating almost every night on the Japanese lines of communication through the area. It is

reliably estimated that the party to which (Sergeant) Sartin belonged (total strength of three), effected the following damage on the enemy: five to eight trains derailed, four large bridge abutments damaged, nine small railway girder bridges destroyed, sixty to seventy rail cuts, nine road craters, four to five hundred telephone wires cut, seven to ten motor transport destroyed and five hundred to one thousand Japanese killed. (Sergeant) Sartin was primarily responsible for executing these demolitions, which were carried out under most difficult circumstances, and on numerous occasions was involved in fighting at close quarters against considerable odds. His skill, courage and devotion to duty during these actions were in a large measure responsible for the success achieved by the small outnumbered patrol to which he belonged'.

Unfortunately John was captured with others by the Japanese on 14 March 1942 and was held in horrendous conditions at Pudu jail in Kuala Lumpur. Several men decided to escape but John declined. It was a decision that saved his life because they were all re-captured and executed. He stayed at Pudu until October 1942 whereupon he was transferred to Nong Pladuk and held there until February 1945, when he was sent to Ubon.

Melvin Henry Mahlandt – US Navy

Melvin Mahlandt was born on 7 August 1916. He joined the United States Navy on 23 August 1937. He subsequently became a Fire Controlman 1st Class on board the USS *Houston*. On the 28 February 1942, the USS *Houston* was sunk (along with HMAS *Perth*) in a fierce battle against the Japanese Navy in the Sundra Straits. Men were fighting for their lives in the open sea. Some of them managed to scramble into life rafts, but these quickly became overcrowded. Strong currents took them away into open seas but they battled hard and, although many drowned, the survivors eventually found land on to which they hauled their weary bodies. They had been in the sea for almost twenty hours. Many were suffering from severe burns and other serious injuries. Even on land there was unpredictability about the friendliness of the inhabitants and uncertainty about Japanese occupation.

The USS *Houston* carried 1,061 men but only 368 survived. Eventually all the survivors were captured and, on 1 March 1942, Melvin's record shows he entered Serang camp in Batavia. He was held there until 13 April 1942 when he was transferred to Bicycle Camp. One month later, Prisoners from the 131st Field Artillery joined them and Melvin probably met Thomas Whitehead, who was also a Prisoner at Ubon. He was transferred to Changi in Singapore on 16 October 1942 and then shipped to Moulmein in Burma on 17 January 1943.

Melvin worked on the Thailand-Burma railway and spent one or two months at Nike camp as an 'automobile mechanic'. From 3 April 1944, he was held in captivity at Nong Pladuk before his transfer to Ubon.

When Melvin entered Ubon camp he had already suffered from malaria, pellagra and a septic nose, and his eyesight was reported to be bad. Fortunately, he is not listed in Ubon's medical diary meaning that his health whilst in the camp was satisfactory.

Lieutenant Cornelis B. Evers – Royal Dutch Army
In 1936, when tension increased on the Dutch border with Hitler's Germany, Lieutenant Evers was drafted into the Dutch Army Border Guards. However, in 1939 he was posted to Surabaya in Java as an officer in the Anti-Aircraft Artillery Corps of the Dutch Colonial Army. His lifestyle at this time was relaxed and he enjoyed a good social life, but this changed abruptly when the Japanese landed at the north of Surabaya on 1 March 1942. One week later the Dutch Army announced that the force of 125,000 men had disbanded.

A large number of the Dutch troops were Moluccan nationals who could easily have disposed of their uniforms and merged into the local villages to remain undetected and avoid becoming Prisoners of War. However, most of them decided to remain loyal to the Dutch Crown and surrendered with the European Dutch to the Japanese. In October 1942 Cornelis was moved to

Tanjong Priok in Batavia and from there to Singapore, where he was imprisoned at Changi.

In January 1943, he was assigned to a group of almost 600 of his compatriots and travelled by rail to Thailand to start work on the railway. Cornelis taught himself to speak Japanese; when he became confident enough, he acted as interpreter between the Japanese and the Allied officers.

Whilst at the 'Hindato' (Hindat) camp, he acted as interpreter for Major Chida, who later became the commandant of the Ubon camp. Major Chida officiated at several funerals and Cornelis had to translate his rather long and laborious speeches into English and Dutch. The problem was that Cornelis could not understand Major Chida's thick accent but he solved this by making up his own version of the Major's utterings. To his surprise, no one noticed the difference!

CSM Joseph Frederick Sawyer – British Army
The announcement that CSM Joseph Sawyer had been awarded the Military Medal is found in the *London Gazette* of 1 August 1946. His citation reads:

288 Field Company, R.E., were employed forward of Balastier Road, Singapore, between 12th and 15th February 1942 both as Sappers and Infantrymen. Throughout this time Company Sergeant Major Sawyer's conduct was of the highest order. Not only did he show initiative and a complete disregard for personal danger, but by his example and courage in maintaining his duties under shell fire, he inspired all men under him to do the same. In addition to his normal duties he evacuated wounded while under fire. When the Company Headquarters was hit on 15th February 1942, he personally supervised the moving of wounded and the re-organisation of HQ. During the whole period he acted as second-in-command of the company and performed the duties of an officer in a most capable way. He supported his Commanding Officer in the highest possible manner at all times.

Private Len Knott– British Army

Private Knott joined the Royal Army Medical Corps at the age of twenty-three. He was posted to Singapore where he worked as medical orderly and pharmacy assistant at the Alexander Military Hospital. He was in the hospital on 14 February 1942 when Japanese soldiers entered the grounds. They ignored the white flag outside the entrance and surged through the corridors where men lay on stretchers waiting for surgery. The hospital personnel were unarmed and wearing Red Cross armbands, but the deranged Japanese took no notice and attacked them with bayonets, resulting in the murder of innocent men. On the operating table was Corporal Bill Holden of the 2nd Loyals, undergoing surgery; he was also murdered.

About two hundred men, including the sick and dying, were forced into groups of four or five and bound together. They were taken to a building in the hospital grounds, and fifty to sixty men were crammed into its small rooms. During the night and the following morning, the Japanese ordered small groups of four or five out of the rooms. As they came outside they were bayoneted to death but, before the Japanese could finish, a bomb scored a direct hit on the building and blew the doors off all of the rooms. Eight men managed to escape. Unfortunately five were shot and killed, but Private Knott was one of the three escapees. Although he got away, he was soon captured and imprisoned in Changi.

By November 1942 he was working in the hospital at Nong Pladuk and remained there until he was moved to Ubon in February 1945, where he was assigned to the camp's hospital.

Gunner William Wilder– British Army

Gunner Wilder was a very talented artist and spent much of his time in the camps drawing and painting. Whilst in Changi, his talent was recognised and he was commissioned to draw the Shinto Shrine, which the men at Changi were forced to build to commemorate Japanese war dead. When men from his unit were transferred to the railway in October 1942, William stayed in Singapore as the unofficial 'Sketchee Man'.

Later, in March 1943 he was moved to Thailand and sent to work on the Wampo Viaduct. Following severe bouts of illness, he was transferred to the hospital camp at Chungkai where he stayed for five months before moving to Nong Pladuk and subsequently to Ubon in February 1945.

Private Thomas Whitehead – US Army

Thomas joined the 131st Field Artillery US Army in Texas just before his seventeenth birthday. He trained as a driver/mechanic, which was to be an advantage when he was held as a Prisoner of War. As he progressed through his training, Thomas thought he was bound for the war in Europe. He never considered fighting in South East Asia and at most he thought he would be away from home for less than a year.

On 11 November 1941 he travelled to San Francisco where he boarded the *USS Republic*, which was bound for the Philippines via Honolulu, Hawaii. On 29 November the ship left Honolulu in a convoy with six other vessels. On 7 December the Japanese attacked Pearl Harbour, Honolulu. The *USS Republic* was immediately put onto a war footing and repainted, whilst at sea, with grey camouflage. They were directed to Fiji whilst discussions about their destination took place. They were almost sent back to Pearl Harbour, but the White House decided to send them onto Brisbane, Australia as the Task Force South Pacific.

After spending Christmas in Brisbane, Thomas and his unit were transferred to Surabaya, in Java to support the United States Air Force by loading bombs and servicing aircraft at Singosari airfield. The Japanese frequently bombed the area, forcing the Air Force to leave in early March. Thomas and his unit moved to the west of Java to defend what they could against the advancing Japanese.

In the event, they did not engage the enemy and surrendered on 9 March 1942. It was the first time the soldiers had come face to face with the Japanese. Thomas described them as '*ragged, shaggy, ill dressed and ill equipped.*' He realised escape was futile because his unit had no knowledge of the island, no food, no weapons and feared the Japanese did not give escapees a second chance.

After being held at Tanjong Priok in Batavia, he was moved to Bicycle Camp and then to Changi. In January 1943 he was sent by train to Georgetown in Malaya where he boarded the Japanese ship *Maru Maru*, which was in a convoy bound for Moulmein in Burma to begin working on the railway from the Burma side. The convoy came under heavy attack from Allied air forces. One ship was sunk and many Dutch Prisoners and Japanese soldiers lost their lives. Despite being damaged, the *Maru Maru* managed to complete its voyage. After a short stay in Moulmein prison the men walked out to 18 Kilo Camp to start work on the railway.

During captivity, Thomas developed dry beriberi caused by a lack of vitamins and developed a serious ulcer that nearly resulted in the amputation of his leg. By November 1943 Thomas was in Chungai hospital camp, where his ulcer was scraped out without any anaesthetic. Eventually he was sent to Nong Pladuk with two soldiers from the 131st, Albert Smoke and Vincent Vogt, and Melvin Mahlandt from the Navy. They were the only Americans to be sent to Ubon.

PART 3

THE WAR IN UBON COMES TO AN END

Chapter 13

THE ALLIES

In December 1941 Luang Phibul's cabinet had consented to allow the Japanese free passage into Thailand. There was overnight political opposition and disbelief amongst the nation. Almost immediately Luang Pridi gathered his most loyal supporters and began to coordinate a resistance movement, which was eventually called the Seri Thai. They determined upon four objectives: to reduce the power and influence of Luang Phibul's government and policies with Japan; to encourage sabotage tactics on Japanese targets; to promote propaganda campaigns, and, most importantly, to contact the Allies as soon as possible to propose mutual support against the Japanese.

Luang Pridi and others who were vehemently opposed to Luang Phibul's decision were quickly moved into positions where their opposition was effectively impotent. Luang Pridi was appointed as one of the three eminent Prince Regents who advised and made decisions on behalf of the young King Rama VIII (Ananda Mahidol), who was attending school in Switzerland. In this distinguished role he kept a relatively low political profile, which allowed him to work secretly to establish the Seri Thai Movement.

Over the next two years Luang Phibul held the balance of power and, as Field Marshall, he had the full support of the army. He retained a close working relationship with the Japanese but, according to Sir Josiah Crosby (former British Minister in Thailand), his premiership degenerated into *'nothing short of a military dictatorship'*.

By the first half of 1944, the military, the police and the nation had lost faith in him as a leader and their patience with the Japanese was waning. In the background the Seri Thai were surreptitiously growing in strength and confidence, boosted by making contact with OSS trained agents who had successfully infiltrated Thailand.

On 1 August 1944 Luang Phibul was ousted as prime minister and replaced by the popular Luang Khuang Aphaiwong. Luang Aphaiwong privately despised the Japanese but outwardly remained on good terms with them so that they did not suspect any antipathy from him. Crucially, he was a close confidant of Luang Pridi who, in his position as Prince Regent, was instrumental in his appointment.

The new cabinet was composed of those who covertly supported the Seri Thai and had high personal integrity, upon which the new prime minister (and Luang Pridi) could rely. True to form, the Japanese demanded another loan to finance their presence in Thailand, but the new Thai government refused to grant it. The message was clear: the Thais were turning against the Japanese; more importantly, this was a positive message to the Allies that Thailand was no longer in a mood to assist Japan. Luang Pridi started to hope that the Allies would gain confidence that the Seri Thai in particular could play a crucial role in the war against Japan.

Meanwhile the groups of Thai expats living and studying in Great Britain and the United States had been trained by their respective hosts' specialist army forces to infiltrate Thailand. Their tasks were to gather intelligence and make contact with active resistance movements.

The British government would not co-operate until, at the very least, the Thai government was seen to *'work their passage'* towards the defeat of the Japanese. The British were angry because the Thai government had allowed Japan into their country, which directly led to the invasion of their colonies in Malaya, Singapore and Burma, countries which were subsequently lost. In addition, Thailand was effectively at war with Great Britain. Politically, it is understandable that the British government was unreceptive to the idea of a *'free Thailand'* after the war ended. As the aggrieved party, it felt entitled to compensation.

Meanwhile, undaunted by the politics but motivated by their loyalty to serve their country, Thai expats living in England were designated enemy aliens and appropriated to the Pioneer Corps. They soon became frustrated and believed their honest intention to rid Thailand of the Japanese was being impeded. A lifeline was provided by the SOE who, like their American OSS counterparts, recognised that Thai nationals could blend easily into Thailand without suspicion. In January 1943 thirty-seven Thai expats were transferred to the SOE; of these, twenty-three were selected for further training in India and Ceylon. By early 1944 they were ready to be deployed into Thailand.

The SOE was responsible for irregular warfare consisting of working behind enemy lines, often with resistance groups, to gather intelligence and sabotage enemy assets and movements. It was a dangerous job and required special skills from special men. As with all British military establishments, the SOE had a strict and often confusing hierarchical structure. They were present in the European and Middle Eastern theatres of war, but in 1943 it was decided to open a section to take responsibility for the South East Asian area. It was named Force 136 and its HQ was established at Kandy in Ceylon under the command of SEAC (South East Asia Command). Force 136 was further divided into country sections with the Siam (Thailand) Country Section (SCS) controlling the Thai agents previously trained in Great Britain.

Even though British political difficulties remained unresolved, there was an appetite from the military to make contact with any potential Thai resistance movement. In June 1943, Major Peter Pointon MC was appointed head of SCS and established his HQ in Calcutta. For the next nine months various operations were set up to infiltrate Thailand and attempt to make contact with resistance movements. Not every operation was successful, and sadly there was loss of life, which did nothing to gain the confidence and support from those, mainly politicians in London, who doubted the value of the SCS. However, by August 1944 SOE-trained agents managed to covertly establish themselves in Bangkok and make contact with the Seri Thai command.

The small number of Thai university students based in the United States did not want to return to Thailand and live under the oppressive Japanese. They eagerly joined the fledgling Free Thai Movement founded by Ambassador M.R. Seni Pramoj. The Americans did not accept Thailand's declaration of war, neither did they have any colonial interests connected with the Thai jurisdiction. Because these barriers did not exist, they were more amenable than the British to suggestions that the students could potentially infiltrate Thailand to spy on their real enemy, the Japanese.

The students were assigned to the newly established OSS, which was similar in purpose to the SOE. They trained vigorously to bring their fitness levels up to an acceptable operational standard and received instruction in jungle survival, guerrilla tactics and intelligence gathering. A year later, the OSS had gained an advantage over the SOE and had trained agents ready to infiltrate Thailand but they would have to wait for the appropriate opportunity.

In March 1943, a group of twenty-one Thai agents left the United States for an OSS camp in north-east India. After further training, they moved to the OSS headquarters at Chungking in southern China. Chungking was a busy hub for all Allied intelligence units. Unfortunately communication between these units became confused; this, together with adverse weather conditions, prevented positive operational progress for the group of Thai agents.

In an attempt to make progress they transferred to Kunming in November 1943 but delay followed them until at last, in February 1944, the first group of five men was divided into three teams and made ready to move. They entered Thailand through northern Laos.

Sadly, one team was captured and killed by the Thai police, who mistook them for bandits. The local Thai police were going about their ordinary business but Japanese curiosity was raised and they discovered the agents were equipped with radios. They suspected they had come into Thailand from Laos and deduced they were enemy agents. After such a long delay, this was a huge early setback for the OSS.

This information found its way to Luang Pridi and for the first time he became aware that attempts were being made to penetrate Thailand by external forces possibly friendly towards a free Thailand. He contacted General Adul, Thailand's Chief of Police, who was sympathetic towards Thailand's anti-Japanese movement. Secret instructions were sent to all police units to send captured agents to his Bangkok office without informing the Japanese. The protocol between the Thai police and the Japanese army was that they should each retain their own captured Prisoners and share information or details about them. The next two OSS teams were 'captured' by the Thai police and surreptitiously conveyed to Bangkok. The agents were unaware that they were in safe hands until General Adul himself interviewed them and revealed that they had reached Thailand's internal resistance movement.

One of the 'captured' agents was Khun Karun Kengradomying. To make Kun Karan's identification easier, he was given the nickname Ken. He was the son of Luang Kat Songkhram, a Royal Thai Air Force officer and an important politician who was involved in Thailand's coup d'état in 1932. Ken created an excellent impression amongst the Seri Thai leaders in Bangkok. During his time there, he gathered important intelligence and made contact with several leading Seri Thai members, including Nai Tiang Sirikhandra from Sakhon Nakhon in north-east Thailand. Nai Tiang was an Assemblyman, or member of parliament, in the Thai government.

In November 1944, Ken returned to Kunming and confirmed the good news that Luang Pridi and General Adul were organising an intelligence network. He brought back the message that Luang Pridi had requested weapons in readiness to rise up against the Japanese. After his debrief in Kunming, Ken was despatched to Washington DC to deliver Luang Pridi's request directly to the OSS command. He made a good impact and, as a result, the OSS gained confidence that the Thailand-based Seri Thai resistance movement was a reliable source that could provide intelligence and be trained to carry out sabotage. The ability of the Seri Thai to actually fight the Japanese was more doubtful but it was assumed that, with proper training, they might be capable of providing useful back up.

Following his return to Thailand, Ken was sent to Ubon to gather intelligence. An application to extend the intelligence network in the Ubon area was forwarded to the British command in April 1945 and included a request for a W/T (wireless/telegraph) station, which was possibly intended for Ken.

Ken stayed at the home of Nai Thong In Phuriphat, the leader of the Seri Thai Movement in Ubon. Nai Thong In was also an Assemblyman and, at the time, the Minister of Education. He was a close associate of Luang Pridi and a firm friend of Nai Tiang Sirikhandra.

Nai Thong In had a daughter called Khun Ora In Phuriphat. She was twelve years old when Ken stayed at the family home. She remembers him working in an upstairs room transmitting messages in Morse code. He was most likely reporting intelligence on the Ubon area to the OSS HQ at Chungking. Her father kept his role in the Seri Thai a secret from her and it was some time later that she learned of his involvement and commitment. The Ubon Seri Thai practised firearms techniques at a secret location, and she remembers one occasion in which a training exercise involving a machine gun went sadly wrong when it accidently fired as it fell off its mounting. She recalls that seven or eight trainees were killed and their bodies quickly buried to avoid discovery by the Japanese.

No official records were kept but Major Hedley a British officer in the SOE, who arrived in Ubon in September 1945, recalls that he attended the proper funerals of deceased men associated with the Seri Thai in Ubon and was told how they had met their demise. The training exercise was in the use of loading and firing a Bren gun. The instructor foolishly sat his men in front of the gun and, to add realism to the exercise, decided to use live ammunition. He demonstrated loading the magazine, placing it in the gun, cocking the gun and then, in a moment of madness, fired the gun. Unfortunately, the safety catch was not in the lock position and the gun went off in automatic mode. Eight members of his class were killed in front of him.

Major Hedley recalls that the funeral was held at a Buddhist temple and was very well attended. Each of the eight open coffins was placed on its own funeral pyre made of heavy logs. During the service, eight ex-Seri Thai guerrillas came forward and stood over a coffin. On command, they fired a three-gun salute to represent the service each of the deceased had given to the Seri Thai Movement. Following the salute, the attending monks were presented with new robes. Close family then anointed the bodies with coconut oil to accelerate the ignition of the fire. This was followed by an invitation to mourners to place a joss stick in each coffin. The Governor and the local judge threw small coins into the crowd of mourners. There was a joyful scrum of children scrabbling to collect the money. Finally, slabs of plastic explosive were set off, creating very loud explosions to mark the end of the service. The pyres were set alight later that evening in private family cremations to the accompaniment of more loud explosions. The following morning all that remained were the ashes from eight fires including fragments of bone. Close family members selected several bone fragments from their deceased relative's ashes and placed them into an urn, which was then buried in the temple's grounds. Today's Buddhist funerals in Thailand follow a similar pattern with many temples now having crematoriums with a simple furnace. However, in poorer villages the funeral pyre is still used.

Although there is no official confirmation, Ken may have also infiltrated the prison camp. He was certainly well trained by the OSS and had the skill and experience to do so. Some Prisoners remembered an unidentified Thai entering the camp on several occasions and acting in an unusual way.

Charles Steel recorded that he knew of messages being passed into and out of the camp to *'non-descript Thais'*. Fergus Anckorn wrote that on one occasion a Thai male strolled into his hut carrying a gun. He and his fellow Prisoners did their best to ignore him, but nevertheless they were very concerned about his intentions. The man asked for five men to be trained in the use of a Bren gun, but Fergus and his comrades suspected a trap and did not react. Fergus said the man left and was never seen again. Maybe Ken was involved in these covert operations.

Soldaat Henk Gideonse writes at length about a person he called the *'Red Ant'* whom he describes as parachuting into Nong Pladuk camp with an English lieutenant and sergeant at the time of the bombardment. He understood their instructions were to build a secret airstrip near Ubon and organise a popular army. Henk's story cannot be verified; however, British SOE officers Major David Smiley and Sergeant Collins parachuted into Sakhon Nakhon in the north of north-east Thailand (details below). Nong Pladuk is in the west of Thailand on the Thailand-Burma railway near Kanchanaburi, and about four hundred and fifty miles from Ubon. Major Smiley did, in fact, liberate the Ubon camp and his final report refers to a *'Red Ant'* whom he identifies as an OSS agent who had been in contact with Nai Tiang Sirikhandra and the Ubon camp.

Finally, in his brief notes on Ubon Dutch Prisoner M. Soesman also refers to a '*Siamese leader*' with an assumed name of the '*Red Ant*'. He was from Ubon and brought news into the camp. It is possible that several Seri Thai agents infiltrated the camp, so whether these stories relate to Ken will never be known.

Throughout 1944, without any political constraints holding them back, the OSS trained agents contacted the Seri Thai and saw no reason why they could not provide support and training. Meanwhile, the SOE were frustrated by the British government's political intransigence. But after top-level discussions between the government and the military, political obstacles were temporarily put aside in favour of the obvious military objective to defeat the Japanese.

The British SCS was authorised to contact the Seri Thai and secretly embed agents in Bangkok to establish consistent lines of communication with Calcutta. In December 1944, Lord Louis Mountbatten, Supreme Commander of the South East Asia Command, was granted permission from the British government to request a meeting with Luang Pridi at Kandy. Luang Pridi viewed this positively but, when he learned that political discussions, especially regarding post-war settlements, were excluded from the agenda, he declined the invitation. There was a suspicion held by the United States and the Seri Thai that the British were reluctant to let go of their colonial ambitions in south-east Asia, and that Thailand maybe a part of their aspirations in a post-war settlement.

In January 1945 the OSS, with the full support of the United States government, arranged a similar meeting with Luang Pridi in Bangkok with an open agenda. This meeting was successful for both sides and finally the OSS was committed to assist the Seri Thai. An agreement to supply arms and training to Seri Thai units throughout Thailand was reached. From this point on, the pace of progress between the OSS and the Seri Thai increased significantly and the British SOE were rapidly falling behind. Somewhat aggravated by the favourable outcome achieved by the Americans, the British once more invited the Seri Thai

115

leadership to meet in Kandy. This time there was more success. Possibly encouraged by the American initiative, the Thai delegation confidently presented the same documents they had discussed with the Americans. Their diplomatic skills convinced the British of their capability to *'work their passage'*, but there was still no discussion about Thailand's post-war independence. This was not surprising following a frank and honest discussion between Thai Foreign Minister Luang Direk Jayanama and Sir Andrew Gilchrist from the SCS, in which Sir Andrew eloquently explained the British position;

'I told him that if he approached us in a bargaining spirit (i.e. regarding independence post war) he was making a big mistake. I recalled that Siam had signed a non-aggression pact with us (Great Britain) in 1941, that she had failed to resist the Japanese in December of that year, in spite of a personal message from Mr. Winston Churchill to the Siamese Premier, but had rather facilitated their attack on our forces in Malaya and Burma, and that a few weeks later she had actually declared war on us and was even now in military occupation of some portions of British territory. It was true, I said, that people like myself and Sir Josiah Crosby (British minister in Bangkok in 1941), who knew the inner facts of the situation and the difficulties and dangers with which the Siamese were confronted, might feel inclined to sympathise and make allowances. But for busy men like Mr. Winston Churchill and for the British public at large, the situation must be judged on the basis of known facts and the facts were somewhat damning.'

The Thai delegation's resistance planning was presented to the British contingent and subsequently approved. The change in the British government's attitude was encouraged by the Seri Thai leadership's commitment and Luang Pridi's personality and dedication, but also there was a realisation that the Japanese were facing defeat as they continued to retreat from Burma. The opportunity for SEAC to close in and defeat the Japanese had arrived. On the 12 January 1945 an SOE application to initiate operation *'Candle'* in north-east Thailand, which includes Ubon, was proposed and approved.

Chapter 14

THE BEGINNING OF THE END

Major Sydney Hudson of Force 136 was sent undercover to liaise with Seri Thai leaders and assess the general situation in Thailand. He had previously worked for the SOE behind enemy lines in France throughout the Normandy campaign in June 1944. The following is an extract from his report.

Thailand is relatively thinly populated and with poor communications. With the exception of one or two large towns it is an agricultural country.
The Japanese occupation, except in certain definite areas is very thin indeed.
The general attitude of the Siamese is anti-Japanese.
The government is really a government of the Resistance Movement.
Outside of the government there are anti-Japanese elements notably the Chinese Secret Society.
The majority of the armed services are definitely anti-Japanese.
The police favour the Resistance Movement and do not collaborate with the Japanese counter espionage service.
The Japanese CE (Counter Espionage) Service does not and cannot exercise any direct control on the Siamese other than at certain vital spots in areas of military importance.
We already possess radio contact with Luang Pridi who apparently combines the position of Regent with that of head of Resistance.
Up till now there have been very few hostile acts against the Japanese.
The Resistance Movement, though widespread, is not really organised for action or perhaps even in such a way as to allow it to make concrete preparations for such actions.

Additional intelligence reports from the same period identified that approximately 12,000 men of the 37th Division of the Royal Thai Army, commanded by Major-General Hansongkram, were stationed in north-east Thailand. One Infantry Regiment belonging to the 37th was stationed in Ubon but the number of men is unknown. The total strength of the Thai Army in Thailand at the time was estimated at 100,000, with 70,000 of those combat ready. There were an estimated 50,000 Japanese troops but the numbers varied as troops retreated from Burma.

The Candle operational area was officially defined as: *'That part of north-east Thailand bounded on the west by the railway running north from Korat to Udon Thani and the road onto Nong Khai, on the north and east by the Mekong River and on the south by the railway from Korat to Ubon'*. It covered an area of 30,000 square miles of forest with few roads but criss-crossed by many tracks and paths only accessible by Jeep or on horseback.

The proposed tasks for the SOE were to establish radio contact with India and to establish liaison at HQ with local Seri Thai units. In addition, they were to organise and train guerrilla patrols, to collect and report military and political intelligence from the area, and to reconnoitre and report drop zones for future sorties. The operational details were approved on 17 January 1945 and preparations began.

To the west of Candle was another operational area code named Coupling. These areas shared the boundary from Korat to Nong Khai. Activities in Coupling broadly followed those of Candle, and occasionally they shared resources. Major Hudson was assigned to this area.

Ubon is located in the south-eastern corner of Candle. When the area was defined, the Ubon camp had not been established and the northern town of Sakhon Nakhon was chosen as Candle's base. This was the hometown of Nai Tiang Sirikhandra. He was the Assemblyman (Member of Parliament) for Sakhon Nakhon and close friend of Luang Pridi, who appointed him leader of the Seri Thai in north-east Thailand.

Nai Tiang was well educated and came from a wealthy family. He was dedicated to his constituency, where his highly principled views on democracy made him a popular leader. He was a fierce opponent of the Phibul government, and condemned Phibul as a collaborator with the Japanese. Nai Tiang was present at Luang Pridi's first meeting that led to the founding of the Seri Thai Movement. The Japanese viewed him with such suspicion that in 1944 Luang Pridi suggested he return to Sakhon Nakhon, keep a low profile and work quietly on setting up the Seri Thai in his area. Using his extensive network of contacts, he made great progress and quickly raised a force of hundreds of men.

Nai Tiang gained a government contract to construct a new road between Sakhon Nakhon province and Kalasin. This project provided perfect cover for Seri Thai training camps and covert DZs for the British Royal Air Force to drop supplies of arms and equipment by parachute. On 27 January 1945, Force 136 supplied Nai Tiang (who had been given the code name of Pluto) with a W/T (wireless/telegraph) station (code name Chiffon), together with an experienced operator called Khun Krit Totsayanon (code name Kong).

Khun Krit Totsayanon was an SOE-trained agent who had infiltrated Thailand in September 1944 at Hua Hin (on the coast south west of Bangkok). His first assignment was to organise reception parties for the delivery of arms and equipment from British Airborne Operations and smuggle them into Bangkok, from where they were distributed to various regional Seri Thai cells. He had an excellent reputation and quickly developed a good relationship with Nai Tiang Sirikhandra.

Nai Tiang Sirikhandra was given a directive by Force 136, which was delivered with the first consignment of arms and explosives. He was under strict instructions that these should only be used for training his men and he should not, under any circumstances, skirmish with the Japanese. The directive did state that the day would come for the Seri Thai to attack the Japanese and *'the north-east may easily become an important centre of operations'*, but first they were to identify suitable places to establish roadblocks and strategic positions to place explosives, such as road and railway bridges. After training, they were to ambush, demolish and sabotage Japanese lines of communication.

To help him gather useful intelligence, Nai Tiang was provided with maps and instructions to accurately identify Japanese positions, paying particular attention to troop numbers and movements on road, rail and airfields. In March, Nai Tiang reported that a landing strip was available at Donhan *[sic]* military aerodrome, fifty miles west north west of Khon Kaen and an airstrip thirty-four miles south west of Lao Phon Kao *[sic]* was under construction.

Nia Tiang was also directed to target specific groups in the area with propaganda produced by Force 136. This was a common tactic; Force 136 worked constantly on ideas to produce disinformation and confusion. One such scheme was to distribute boxes of matches with anti-Japanese messages printed on them. It was thought that matches, which were known to be in short supply in Thailand, would be useful and hopefully carry the propaganda over a wide area. However, the scheme to produce them was almost a disaster for the officers at Siam Country Section.

The idea emanated from SCS HQ and a lot of thought went into the design of the box, which had a picture of a young Thai girl alongside the slogan *'Death to the Japanese'*. Through connections within the SCS, a manufacturing order was placed with the Swedish Match Company based in India. Tens of thousands of boxes, complete with matches, were produced but the Indian government would not release them until the tax levied on matches was paid in full. This caused a problem for SCS because they did not have the budget to pay the tax. The matches were finally released on the production of a document purporting to be signed by Lord Mountbatten which, of course, was a fake.

Be that as it may, the matches were released and distribution throughout Thailand began. However, when it came to actual payment for the matches and the tax, the SCS were somewhat embarrassed because not only had they failed to obtain permission from HQ to proceed with the original order, neither did they have the money with which to pay the Swedish Match Company and the Indian government. The creditors were demanding £7,000 and threats of a court martial began to circulate the office.

Just when SCS were fearing the worst, the situation was saved by the unlikely intervention of Thai minister Luang Direk Jayanama. At a meeting with HQ, whilst discussing collaboration between Great Britain and Thailand, he was asked about the effectiveness of propaganda and replied that the matchboxes were a brilliant idea and people were even selling them! As a result of his comment, payment was duly authorised without further investigation and SCS had ridden their luck!

The second group targeted with propaganda was the Royal Thai Army. They received a leaflet with messages to *'win them over'*. Nai Direk commented that, in his opinion, these had been a waste of time.

Force 136 sent a 'miniature' Roneo printing machine to the Candle operation for producing local propaganda messages and other uses, such as issuing orders and training instructions. There was a message to say a larger machine was available if required.

Nai Tiang was supported by every town governor and established training centres in Khon Kaen, Mahasarakham, Nong Khai, Phanna Nikhom, and Sakhon Nakhon. Volunteers enthusiastically came forward from the villages, particularly teachers and civil servants.

Although there were few Japanese units in the area performing routine duties, they realised that Thai attitudes were turning against them and were aware of the formation of Seri Thai resistance groups. They sent search parties to look for suspected guerrilla activity and requested (demanded) assistance from each town's governor, police chief and army officers. However, unbeknown to the Japanese, these officials were now embedded in the Seri Thai network. They gave the Japanese confusing directions and false information which bought time for the Seri Thai to evacuate and cover up their positions.

From mid-March 1945, British RAF Liberators specially adapted for long range flights started to drop more consignments into the Candle area for the Seri Thai. Inevitably, despite agreeing not to overlap their operations, there was occasional confusion between the SOE and OSS. At a meeting between the SOE and OSS held on 20 April, the OSS stated they were sending an officer, Major John Holladay, with a radio operator into the Candle area in the first week of May. In reply, the SOE confirmed that one of their officers was to be posted into the Candle area. It made no difference; Major Holladay was dropped close to Sakhon Nakhon on 12 May 1945 and was greeted by Nai Tiang and Khun Amnuai Phunphiphat (nick name Amney) who had been trained by the OSS in the United States. He established his camp at Ban Nong Luang which is north west of Sakhon Nakhon. Major Holladay's orders were restricted to investigating the potential to gather intelligence and, if feasible, organising an intelligence network. He was told to leave Seri Thai training to SOE Force 136 personnel.

Major John Holladay's code name was Sleeve. He was a stocky, genial man in his fifties. Fifteen years prior to the outbreak of the war, he had worked in Thailand as a Presbyterian missionary and with some success as a doctor. Before working in Thailand, he spent thirteen years in China. At the outbreak of the war, he left Thailand and returned to the United States. When he was contacted by the OSS as part of their 'Moral Operations' scheme, which loosely implied 'black psychological warfare', he volunteered to fight against the Japanese and in April 1945 he returned to Thailand.

Major Holladay was fluent in Thai and familiar with Thailand's customs and culture. He established a medical clinic at Ban Nong

Luang which concealed intelligence gathering and resistance activities. He was assisted by Amney, who was a member of the second group of OSS Thai agents trained in the United States. Although Major Holladay kept a low profile and assiduously gathered intelligence, up to 200 Seri Thai were armed by the OSS to protect him.

At the end of April 1945, the SOE assigned Major David de Crespigny Smiley to the Candle area. Major Smiley was born in 1916. In 1936 he graduated from Sandhurst and was commissioned into the Royal Horse Guards. He had a reputation for the social 'high life' and enjoyed fast cars, flying aircraft and horse riding. In 1943 he was recruited by the SOE and sent to Syria, before going to Albania on operations behind enemy lines. He was awarded the Military Cross for his work with local guerrillas and further actions earned him a bar.

In January 1945 after finishing his tour of duty in Albania, Major Smiley met a family friend and member of the Thai Royal family, Prince Subha Svasti. The prince was a Thai resident living in England when Thailand declared war on Great Britain. Rather than return to Thailand, His Highness joined the fledgling Seri Thai Movement in Britain and the Pioneer Corps. He eventually became an officer in SOE Force 136 Siam Country Section.

After a short discussion with the Prince, Major Smiley, who seemingly was able to make his own decisions on where he was engaged in the war, was enticed by the Seri Thai cause and immediately made the necessary arrangements to confirm his deployment. His wide experience, fearless leadership and acute sense of duty made him the ideal SOE officer to go to Thailand to train and develop the Seri Thai Movement in the north-east of the country.

After a period of leave to attend to personal matters, Major Smiley set out in March 1945 on the first part of the journey to the Far East and Candle just one month short of his twenty-ninth birthday. He arrived in Cairo where he met Major Peter Kemp, his friend and comrade from the Albanian tour. Over a lunch of shish kebab and Turkish coffee, they talked about Thailand and the Seri Thai. Major Kemp's curiosity was aroused, and he readily accepted Major Smiley's invitation to join the Thailand operation.

Major Smiley travelled on to the SOE HQ in Kandy and, after completing an intensive two-week training course on jungle tactics and survival, he transferred to the Siam Country Section HQ at Calcutta. Whilst on the training course, he selected Sudhi Sudisakdi and Santa Sintavi, two SOE-trained Thai nationals, to accompany him to Thailand. They were given the code names of Chat and Pun and apart from being fit, tough and speaking reasonable English, their sense of humour appealed to Major Smiley. Major Smiley was given the code name Grin.

Sergeant Collins, code name Gunner, who came to Major Smiley's attention whilst in Albania, joined the group later. He was an expert radio operator and had exactly the loyalty, courage and resolve required for the Thailand operation.

The operation in the Candle area was part of an ambitious plan being developed by Lord Louis Mountbatten, the Supreme Commander of the South East Asia theatre of war. After losing the battles of Imphal and Kohima in north-east India, the Japanese faced further defeat as the 14th Army, led by the illustrious Field Marshall William Slim, forced their retreat through Burma into Thailand. The concentration of Japanese forces, particularly along the Thailand-Burma railway, made Thailand a strategic target to the Allies. Lord Mountbatten agreed that a well-trained and adequately armed guerrilla army could play an important role in harassing the Japanese. However, when the Americans dropped atom bombs on Hiroshima and Nagasaki in early August 1945, the Japanese surrendered and Lord Mountbatten's plans were scrapped. This also meant that Major Smiley's responsibilities altered significantly but, before that climactic event, there was important work to attend to in the Candle area.

Major Smiley had his first view of the Candle area on 20 May 1945 when he travelled as an observer on a Liberator flight piloted by Wing Commander Hodges from 357 Squadron. This flight was one of many routine supply flights of these workhorse aircraft to Thailand. They were specially adapted by taking out unnecessary weight and fitting additional fuel tanks. This enabled them to fly non-stop over long distances and more than twelve hours from their main base at Jessore in northern India. Major Smiley's flight refuelled at the advanced base at Akyab on the western coast of Burma, which had recently been taken back from the Japanese.

Prior to leaving for Candle, Force 136 gave Major Smiley a long list of tasks he was expected to perform:

Tasks in General
To establish close liaison with F.S.M. (Free Siam Movement (Seri Thai)) through Pluto (Nai Tiang Sirikhandra)).
To assist them in all matters of training and, when necessary, advise them on their tactical role and dispositions.
To assess their demands for stores and advise HQ accordingly.
To explore the possibility of introducing further B.O.s (British Officers) into Candle area, whether in teams or singly.
Tasks in Particular
To guard your security and maintain the clandestine nature of your operation until directed to take action by HQ.
To send all intelligence possible and to grade same as briefed.
To give monthly estimates of effectiveness in your area.
To establish regular W/T (radio contact) with this HQ.
To establish an emergency DZ in a remote area where we can locate you if (a) you are forced to hide (b) you lose W/T contact.
To develop landing strips.
To pass W/T targets suitable for the RAF.
To maintain close relations with PLUTO and KONG , and to take into account their local knowledge and influence when determining and deciding on targets and areas in which eventually to operate.

To examine and report on situation and condition of P.O.W. camps in the area. To advise HQ on the possibility of a coup, at a later stage, aimed at the release of P.O.W..

To locate important L of C (Lines of Communication) targets in area and to arrange for their demolition at a suitable time.

To liaise with the O.S.S. officer and report to HQ Calcutta any decisions that you may make regarding co-operation with him.

To give confidential reports from time to time on the F.S.M. (Seri Thai) stating extent of their co-operation and readiness to accept tasks allotted by this HQ.

To ascertain and report on local reactions to propaganda as hitherto carried out, and to make recommendations for its improvement.

To report on economic situation generally and in particular, giving local prices, shortages, surpluses, movements etc of commodities.

To report on the adequacy of internal communications, particularly telegraphs and W/T. How quickly can Pluto receive messages from Ruth (code name for Luang Pridi)?

To report on the local attitude towards the French.

Major Smiley was also given a letter of introduction to give to Nai Tiang Sirikanda:

The bearer of this letter is the leader of a party consisting of Grin (Major Smiley), Gunner (Sergeant Collins), Chat (Sudhi Sudisakdi) and Pun (Santa Sintavi). He comes to you at the request of your authorities and leaders in Bangkok.

He will advise us of your work and progress and will place at your disposal his experience in the kind of work you are engaged in. We hope that this will be of great assistance both to you and to us against the common enemy.

We shall act on the advice he sends on all matters connected with the supply of stores and equipment of every kind. Please discuss with him in full your wishes and requirements. He will explain to you the conditions and difficulties which affect supply particularly during the monsoon months which have now arrived. It is our wish and intention to send you all reasonable and suitable supplies in the quantities you need.

Please afford him all facilities and protection and safe accommodation and arrange for his movements and introductions to local authorities as may be required.

Between 30 April and 2 May 1945, Brigadier Victor Jacques from the British Army secretly arrived in Bangkok with help from the Seri Thai. He met Luang Pridi to gather updates and discuss plans in each area, including Candle and Coupling. On 29 May, Major Smiley met Brigadier Jacques for a final briefing before boarding a Liberator at the start of his operation. Flight Officer Coy was the pilot and his crew were Canadian. With Major Smiley were Chat, Pun and Gunner. The weather was poor forcing the aircraft to fly at high altitude where they felt the cold, despite the warm clothing they were wearing.

At 05:46 on 30 May they arrived at the drop zone, which was identified by the *'correct reception of 'V' panels and 'T' of smoke fires.'* Major Smiley refers to the drop zone as *'close to the village of Ban Non Han'*. The co-ordinates recorded on the flight log suggest that the drop zone was in an area about four miles to the west of Sakhon Nakhon, close to the aerodrome.

Dr Sawat Sresik in his book *Seri Thai in North-East Thailand* (written in Thai and translated into English) indicates that the drop zone was on the east side of the vast lake, which is located to the east of Sakhon Nakhon. He also states that Major Smiley was taken to the village of Ban Non Hom, which is about ten miles east of Sakhon Nakhon. (Note should also be made of a secret Seri Thai meeting place on the outskirts of Phu Phan National Park, about ten miles south west of Sakhon Nakhon. In 2011 a memorial was erected in the park in honour of Nai Tiang Sirikandra and the Sakhon Nakhon branch of the Seri Thai. Not far from the monument is a secret cave where the Seri Thai held meetings and stored weapons. Although there are no surviving records, it is likely that Major Smiley was aware of the cave and probably visited it several times.)

First to parachute out of the Liberator was Major Smiley. He should have been followed by Chat, then Pun and finally Gunner,

127

but all three failed to exit. It was Chat's first jump and Major Smiley recalls he froze on the launch chute. The pilot made a second circuit and, with some 'persuasion' from Pun, Gunner and the dispatcher, Chat made a successful exit. However, in a second version of the incident it is recorded that Chat's leg became entangled with his static line as he started to go down the chute. The dispatcher grabbed him and hauled him back into the plane. Chat was no doubt shaken and the plane had to circle back to the drop zone. On the second attempt everyone exited safely and landed in the correct place. Major Smiley was especially pleased that the two bottles of whiskey he carried remained intact.

The reception party was led by Nai Tiang and Khun Krit. The men were greeted warmly and made very welcome. Major Smiley instinctively knew that he would be able to trust Nai Tiang. Even so, he recalls it was strange to be 1,000 miles behind enemy lines and 1,500 miles away from base.

In the first few days after his arrival, Major Smiley visited as many of the guerrilla camps as possible. Sergeant Collins established radio contact with Calcutta which henceforth was code named 'Felt'. He was a very skilled radio operator and successfully contacted HQ every day throughout the entire Candle operation. Khun Krit had already set up his radio with the code name 'Chiffon'.

Major Smiley was naturally concerned for his personal security and that of the party, although Nai Tiang was confident it was unlikely they would be disturbed by the Japanese because he knew that there were few of their troops in the area. He believed that his guerrilla forces would easily overpower them if they were discovered. Major Smiley had to remind Nai Tiang of the strict order for everyone to remain undercover. Nai Tiang accepted his mild reproach, but his enthusiasm to fight encouraged Major Smiley. They travelled together extensively throughout the area in either Nai Tiang's two-seater Ford or his utility van. There were no major incidents or encounters with the Japanese.

Major Smiley met Major John Holladay, the American OSS agent who had arrived in the Candle area before him. The meeting went well, and they agreed not tread on each other's toes. Although Major Smiley stayed overnight, there is no evidence of further meetings or contact.

Whilst travelling between Seri Thai camps, it was sometimes easier and safer to ride on horseback through the forests and countryside. As trained military horsemen, Major Smiley and Sergeant Collins were comfortable and enjoyed this option but Chat and Pun, being city dwellers, found riding painful and much less pleasurable.

Nai Tiang was very well connected throughout the Candle area and knew all the officials, most of whom were Seri Thai collaborators. When Major Smiley arrived, there were estimated to be 3,000 trained guerrillas, a working intelligence gathering system was in place and two training camps had been established. The main limitation was an acute shortage of arms and explosives but there was no lack of enthusiasm, and their morale was boosted by Major Smiley's presence.

The first camp they inspected was located south of Sakhon Nakhon in the forested hills surrounding the village of Tao Ngoi. The camp was a designated drop zone code named 'Kempton'. Further south from Tao Ngoi, the Seri Thai constructed an airstrip at Na Khu, which was code named 'Heston'. The original landing strip was deemed too short to accommodate Dakotas and had to be extended. The Assemblyman for the area, Nai Chamlong Daorueang, supervised an enthusiastic and hardworking workforce to lengthen the airstrip to 1,000 yards and a width of fifty yards. The foundations were improved by laying a base of rock nine inches in depth with a top surface of three inches of soil and sand, which was sown with grass.

More than 3,000 local villagers worked non-stop for six weeks on the extension, either quarrying the stone from a site five miles away, or transporting the rock by bullock and cart, or working on the airstrip. It was a tremendous effort that was praised by Major Smiley in his final operations report. On the 12 July a Dakota landed at Heston, but the pilot reported it was soft in places. Consequently no more landings were authorised until the soft sections were re-laid. This was a great disappointment to the people who had worked so hard to make it operable. Although repairs were made, it was only used on two other occasions.

Construction on other airstrips in the Candle area was duly abandoned and other available airstrips in the area were never used because security was inadequate. Heston airstrip was still visible in 2019; it now belongs to the Royal Thai Air Force, although it remains inoperable.

Heston was also a designated as a drop zone. Sadly, on 19 June a Liberator, on its way to drop supplies there was reported missing. There was no trace of the aircraft nor any reported reason why it was missing. It was assumed lost either over Burma or the Bay of Bengal. This was a reminder of the huge risk undertaken by the brave and hardworking air crews when flying on these long operations.

Making contact with the Royal Thai Army was one of many priorities. Most towns had a garrison of sorts, and they could be relied upon if called by the Seri Thai. In his final report, Major Smiley states that the only presence of the Royal Thai Air Force in the Candle area was at Korat, but they had active aerodromes in the adjacent Coupling area. There is no mention of any squadrons or aeroplanes located at Ubon aerodrome, but other intelligence suggests that a small squadron was probably based there. The airworthiness of the Thai aircraft was limited due to a scarcity of spare parts and a shortage of fuel.

On the advice of Nai Tiang, Major Smiley did not have too much contact with the police. This was because there was distrust between Nai Tiang and General Adul, the Chief of Police in Bangkok. Consequently, Nia Tiang did not fully rely upon or trust the local force. Nevertheless, the Sakhon Nakhon police were very helpful when it was necessary to divert the attention of Japanese patrols away from the Seri Thai areas. They also provided reliable intelligence on Japanese movements.

The governors of each town in the area were also reliable and the kingpins of local Seri Thai units, and the governor of Ubon, Luang Narat Raksa, was no exception. They introduced doctors, judges and local civil servants to their local units and provided vital services such as medical, telephone, transport and intelligence. The majority of schools in the area were closed down and the teachers and the older pupils volunteered to join their nearest Seri Thai group. Major Smiley found he had an enthusiastic and willing guerrilla force and reported that he had their fullest co-operation. In his final report he complimented them by writing *'it was to everybody's regret that they never got a chance to show what they could really do'*.

Couriers carried messages between the training camps on motorbikes or by car on the few roads which were in reasonable condition. However, riding horses through the maze of uncharted tracks and paths through dense woodland was safer and helped to avoid detection. It is reported that the Seri Thai constructed more than 200 miles of forest tracks to help them. The condition of the roads damaged motor vehicles but kept the mechanics busy. A shortage of tyres was an additional frustration; eighty-eight tyres of various sorts were requisitioned from Calcutta HQ but only four actually arrived.

Telephone and telegraph systems were available, but the Japanese were known to tap into the lines and this discouraged the Seri Thai from using them extensively. In fact, the only public lines connected Korat with Nakhon Phanom via Udon Thani, and Korat and Nakhon Phanom via Ubon. Field telephones were used to link the camps but each village could pass on warnings and simple messages using drums made from hollow bamboo, especially to announce approaching Japanese.

Major Smiley moved his HQ to a village he called Ban Non Han said to be five miles from Tao Ngoi. It was given the code name 'Ascot.' From there, he could see the distant town of Sakhon

Nakhon and Nong Han lake. Although a local search for the village in 2019 failed to locate it, a camp site close to Tao Ngoi was located from which the views could be seen clearly and it was locally recognised as a Seri Thai camp and drop zone.

Major Smiley commented that the camp had good accommodation, food and entertainment. The friendly and lively atmosphere appealed to him and the 1,000 guerrillas who were being trained there. Ten camps were recorded across the region: Ban Huang Yang; Ban Non Hom; Ban Han; Ban Lao Phon Khamo; Ban Wanon Niwat; Ban Huang Waritchaphun; Ban Tha Bo; Ban Wang Khon Mahasarakham; Ban Michai, and Ban Nong Han.

The number of guerrillas in the Candle area rose to 12,000. They received basic first-stage training in the use of bren guns, rifles, sten guns, carbines and grenades. This was followed by the selection of men who showed potential for advanced training on military tactics. This group was then divided between those showing leadership qualities and those thought good enough to fight the Japanese when, and if, the time came. Many were trained in intelligence gathering to obtain strategic information on Japanese strengths and movements in the area.

Major Smiley proposed two battalions based on each town of Ubon, Sakhon Nakhon and Korat, with one battalion from each town of Mahasarakham, Udon Thani, Nong Khai, Nakhon Phanom and Mukdahan, making eleven battalions in total. Each battalion consisted of five companies and each company had one hundred men. This made a total of 5,500 men but, as Major Smiley later learned, even though the proposal was agreed by HQ, the arms, ammunition and explosives received were only sufficient to equip 1,000 men, which equated to one company. In part this was due to cancelling air drops because of poor monsoon weather, but nevertheless it was very disappointing. In his final report Major Smiley stated that 16,000 guerrillas had been trained across the Candle region.

Increased Seri Thai activity in the countryside raised Japanese suspicions but only one camp was discovered, which was burned to the ground. An airstrip was also tracked down, and the Japanese guarded this for the rest of the war. Major Smiley – and the Seri Thai – were frustrated by the strict order not to attack these guards, who were regarded as easy targets.

A report issued on 6 May indicated that 1,000 British, American, Filipino and Indian Prisoners were being held near Ubon to build a new aerodrome. (It should be noted that Prisoners were arriving at the camp up to June and the final number of men was 3,035.) One of Major Smiley's tasks was to attempt to make contact and assist in any escape attempts. He was aware of the camp when he arrived at Candle, but decided to establish himself in the area first by developing the Seri Thai camps and training.

On 23 June, three weeks after his arrival, he received information that a Seri Thai agent had been in contact with the camp. (This may have been the 'Red Ant' and possibly OSS agent Ken.) He decided to investigate and started his journey by travelling from Ascot to Heston, where he intended to spend the night. After his arrival, word was received that a Japanese patrol was advancing towards the camp and they immediately started to evacuate. Sergeant Collins packed away the wireless transmitter set and gave it to the guerrillas to hide, whilst Major Smiley crammed his code books and secret papers into a special SOE briefcase. The briefcase had a false bottom in which five pounds of thermite was concealed. Hidden batteries connected an activation switch to produce an electric charge, which ignited the thermite and produced an intense burst of high temperature. The heat it created was intended to destroy the briefcase and its contents to prevent the enemy taking possession of them. During his haste to get away, the briefcase prematurely ignited; Major Smiley took the full thrust of the flame and was severely burned about the face, arms, knees and hands. His eyelids fused closed and the skin on his hands burned to the bone. Without intervention and first-aid assistance from Sergeant Collins and Nai Tiang, he would most likely have died.

Despite his injuries, they quickly cleared the camp, but it was soon discovered that the report of an advancing Japanese patrol was a false alarm. On returning to the camp, Major Smiley was given morphia pills to ease the pain but they were ineffective, and throughout the night he shook with an intense fever. With no medication for serious burns, he was given local remedies of coconut oil alternating with the juice from a prickly-pear cactus plant to massage into his burns.

Sergeant Collins contacted Calcutta to arrange an evacuation flight. Unfortunately there was a shortage of suitable aircraft that could land at Heston, even though the airstrip was serviceable for emergencies. It was going to be some time before a flight could be arranged to evacuate the major. Meanwhile his burns turned septic and an infestation of maggots started to eat away at the dead flesh.

After three days, Major Smiley was able to open his eyes but he had difficulty taking food and could not use his hands. He fell into a deep depression and admitted later that he was on the verge of taking his own life. Nai Tiang contacted Luang Pridi, who said he would send a doctor to Heston.

On 30 June, seven days after the accident, a Japanese Nagoya fighter-bomber flew over the airstrip and, thinking they were under attack, everyone ran for cover. When it landed, two Royal Thai Air Force pilots disembarked and asked for Major Smiley; they had orders to take him for medical treatment.

The first leg of the journey took them to another airstrip close to Khon Kaen, some two hundred miles away. After receiving rudimentary treatment there, a Royal Thai Air Force Corsair transferred Major Smiley to the Seri Thai airstrip at Naarn, which was a further one hundred miles west. On 5 July he was taken from Naarn by a Royal Air Force Dakota to Rangoon where, on 6 July, thirteen days after the accident, he at last boarded a flight to Alipore near Calcutta where there was a hospital that could treat his wounds properly.

Major Smiley's society background included friendships, acquaintances and connections with many influential and aristocratic people and families living in India. One such connection in Calcutta was Baron Casey, the governor of Bengal. On hearing that Major Smiley had to recuperate from his injury, he invited him to stay at Government House. Whilst staying in these palatial surroundings, the major met Mahatma Gandhi whom he described as having a '*good sense of humour but looked a little incongruous in the drawing room wearing his dhoti.*'

The climate in Calcutta was intensely hot and Major Smiley readily accepted an invitation from Lady Wavell, the wife of Field Marshall Sir Archibald Wavell who was Viceroy of India between 1943 and 1947, to convalesce at her family home in Simla, where it was much cooler. The change of climate was a great benefit and, whilst there, he attended engagements and participated in activities amongst the social elite. It was a far cry from the conditions in north-east Thailand. When his burns had healed sufficiently, Major Smiley returned to Calcutta to prepare for his return to Thailand and the countryside of Candle.

Whilst Major Smiley was away, the Japanese suspicion about guerrilla activity intensified. There was growing tension amongst the guerrillas who wanted to take the fight to the enemy. Their ambition was tempered by a new order from Supreme Allied Command, which was concerned that Major Smiley's absence would lead to a lapse of discipline and result in '*a premature blow-up in Siam*'. They ordered that all airborne operations to the Candle area must be authorised in triplicate by themselves, Luang Pridi and the drop zone reception party. In addition to the Allied Command's concerns about the Seri Thais' eagerness to fight, there was an unwelcome outbreak of smallpox in the area. An air drop of vaccine was authorised, which helped to bring it under control.

When the Japanese identified the activities of Nai Tiang and Sergeant Collins, they ordered a battalion to Sakhon Nakhon to mount an extensive search for them. The men went into hiding in the countryside and the Japanese, without intimate knowledge of the myriad of tracks and paths criss-crossing the endless woodlands, failed to find them. However, they successfully located three unfinished and unserviceable airstrips. Major Smiley's return was necessary to control the increasingly difficult and tense situation in the Candle area.

At the beginning of August, Major Smiley arrived in Calcutta on his way back to Thailand. Here he met Major Kemp, whom he had met in Cairo and suggested he join the SCS, and Major Winn. They had been assigned to Operation Candle and were preparing for their tour of duty. Their preparations were interrupted, however, by the startling news that on 6 August the Americans had dropped an atom bomb on Hiroshima. There was mounting speculation that this might lead to a Japanese surrender. Then on 9 August another bomb was dropped on Nagasaki, leading to the Japanese surrender on 15 August.

This meant a dramatic change for all SOE and OSS operations in Thailand. The immediate concern was for the safety and welfare of all Allied Prisoners in South East Asia and the Pacific region. They had to be protected at all costs from the possibility of a Japanese reprisal. Major Smiley was also concerned that the Seri Thai, the Thai army and police in the Candle area might launch revenge attacks upon the Japanese. Such actions would inevitably lead to unnecessary mayhem and bloodshed. It was vital that the British officers returned to Candle as quickly as possible.

Majors Kemp and Winn arrived in Candle on 16 August, together with Sergeant Lawson (code name Spider), who was the radio operator for Major Winn, and a Thai interpreter code name Toy. Major Smiley was delayed in Rangoon for two days due to engine trouble with the Dakota in which he was due to fly. When he arrived back at Candle on 18 August, he was immediately greeted by Nai Tiang, Sergeant Collins, Chat and Pun and other senior Seri Thai members. They met at a secret camp in Phanna Nikhom, which is north west of Sakhon Nakhon.

Communication of accurate news and orders was difficult for everyone, including the Japanese. The lack of reliable information created a tense, unpredictable atmosphere that could easily descend into reprisals from both the Japanese and Seri Thai. Although the Japanese announced their surrender on 15 August, official news was slow to filter through to their units in north-east Thailand.

On 17 August, the Japanese were reportedly still searching for and arresting anyone connected with the Seri Thai and the Allies, but on 18 August senior Japanese officers finally received orders to cease fire and move to major towns to await surrender orders and further instructions. It was still impossible to predict how they would react to defeat, however; the SOE officers feared that the Japanese would not surrender peacefully and would possibly turn on the Prisoners in random acts of violence.

After consulting the Candle party, Major Smiley sent Major Kemp to Nakhon Phanom, opposite the French Indochina town of Thakhek on the river Mekong. Major Winn was despatched to Nong Khai, opposite Vientiane which is also on the Mekong. It was known that French civilian internees were being held in the French Indochina towns, but their condition was unknown. It was assumed that they were in danger and had to be liberated safely. This was a difficult task made more demanding by remoteness and a lack of effective communication. Major Kemp set off without a wireless transmitter and had to keep in contact with Major Smiley by sending a courier between Nakhon Phanom and Ubon.

Chapter 15

UBON CAMP LIBERATION

In his biography *Irregular Regular*, Major Smiley remembers that he '*wanted to get to Ubon as quickly as possible.*' However, the number of days between the date he arrived back at Phanna Nikhom on 18 August and arrived in Ubon on 26 August, suggest it took him longer than his urgency suggests.

Ubon is more than 200 miles away from Phanna Nikhom and the roads were difficult. Major Smiley travelled with Nai Tiang who provided the transport and Sergeant Collins, who was responsible for maintaining radio contact with HQ. It is very likely that on his journey he met Seri Thai groups and town governors to discuss local situations, so it is feasible that the journey would have taken at least four or five days. Importantly, Major Smiley was very uncertain about how the Japanese in that remote area would react to meeting British officers and tried to remain hidden throughout the journey.

At Mukdahan, the governor told him that a Japanese colonel commanding two battalions in the town wished '*to surrender to the British officer he has been chasing for the past six months.*' Although keen to accept the Colonel's surrender, Major Smiley ignored the request and, maintaining his cover, continued on his way.

On 24 August, two days before arriving at Ubon, a 'Warning Order' was sent out to all Force 136 officers operating in Thailand. It was headed '*Instructions for parties to enter camps in Siam*' and stated what action officers were authorised to take in the aftermath of the surrender. Before taking any action, they had to remain undercover until they received the code word '*Goldfish*'.

Major Smiley's specific orders were to enter the Ubon camp with Sergeant Collins and set up the wireless transmission station. He should then contact the Prisoners' senior officer and make radio contact with HQ, following the agreed existing broadcast schedules. HQ wanted information about the Prisoners including the number of men being held, their medical condition and the food situation. Major Smiley also had to assess the requirements for additional specialised personnel, for example medical and motor transport professionals. The order specifically stated that the Japanese were to remain in control of the camp until the arrival of Allied military authorities. The final instruction was: *'You are not repeat not empowered (to) accept surrender (of) any repeat any Japanese troops.'*

After leaving Mukdahan, Major Smiley arrived at Yasothon; on his way, he passed columns of Japanese soldiers who were marching towards Ubon. On this occasion he made little attempt to remain hidden but was not challenged. He noted the sullen, defeated looks on the faces of the forlorn Japanese. He was joined by Major Chris Brathwaite, who had arrived from the Coupling area to assist Major Smiley because it transpired there was no Prisoner of War camp in the Coupling area to liberate. They continued to Ubon without incident.

At the time of the surrender, a reasonably large Japanese garrison was stationed at Ubon. When he heard this news, Major Smiley was concerned that appearing unannounced in the town might result in him, Major Brathwaite and their radio operators being shot on sight. In addition, he was well aware that a defeated Japanese soldier would rather kill himself than surrender to an enemy. He obviously wanted to avoid conflict and further tragedy at the end of a long war, so they waited undercover for the *'Goldfish'* codeword. But at the same time, they were anxious to contact the ex-Prisoners to reassure them that plans for their repatriation were underway. Of equal importance was to ensure that the Japanese camp commander, Major Chida, guaranteed the men's safety and treated them with due care and attention.

Without making contact with the camp, the situation could not be properly assessed, nor could action plans be put into effect. In addition, Major Smiley was concerned about the difficult task of the surrender and the disarmament of thousands of Japanese. Against this unpredictable background there was an outbreak of smallpox in Ubon; fortunately it did not reach the camp, although great care and vigilance was obviously essential.

On arrival at Ubon, they contacted Colonel Prom Thong Phad at the Royal Thai Army barracks in Warin Chamrap, just south of the river Mun and close to the railway station. They were told that the Royal Thai Army had already entered the prison camp and obtained an estimate of clothing and food supplies required for the Prisoners. This was a very useful start but Major Smiley needed additional information. He wrote a short note with his questions, which was addressed to the British senior officer in the camp. This was delivered secretly by Colonel Prom Thong Phad.

The following reply, in typically military terms, was returned;

Camp strength
British 1,458
Dutch 1,472
Australian 101
American 4
Total 3,035

Requirements – Clothing etc
4,000 blankets
3,000 pairs of shorts
3,000 shirts
4,000 pairs of boots
10,000 razor blades
3,000 razor blade holders
6 open razors

Medical
50,000 Atabrine[1] tablets
500 GMS (1lb) Yatren[2]
100 ampules of Ephedrine[3] (asthma)

Food
500 tins of milk
Cigarettes and tobacco

Health of Camp
Good in general
Approximately 20 stretcher cases
Approximately 300 sitting cases

Japanese still here. All hoping to welcome you very soon.

I am your obedient servant,

> *E.A. Smyth*
> *Major R.A.M.C.*
> *S.M.O., P.o.W. Camp Ubon*

Following the exchange of notes, Major Smiley and the colonel discussed how they could arrange a secret meeting between a British officer who must remain undercover, and ex-Prisoners who were guarded by unpredictable Japanese soldiers. It was going to be a challenge, but Colonel Prom Thong Phad hatched an excellent plan.

Captain Eric Martin remembers a note being delivered into the camp by Jin, a local Chinese girl who regularly delivered ice and had previously been helpful in passing messages between the camp and the local villagers. The note presumably informed them that three British officers were to attend an important

---

[1] Atabrine was used to treat malaria.
[2] Yatren was used to treat amoebic dysentery.
[3] Ephedrine was used to treat low blood pressure and asthma.

meeting at the Royal Thai Army HQ in Warin Chamrap on some concocted pretext or other.

Colonel Prom Thong Phad sent an escort to collect the officers and bring them to the Warin barracks. Major Smiley was hiding in a room above the officers' mess. From his window, he could see the joint Thai and Japanese guard with the British officers as they arrived. They entered a downstairs room in the officers' mess, where the Colonel deliberately kept them waiting for a long time. Eventually he contrived for each of the officers, accompanied by a Thai guard, to go in turn to the lavatory. The Japanese guards were ordered to remain with the other two officers. Instead of going to the lavatory, each officer was taken to meet Major Smiley in his upstairs hiding place.

The three officers were Major E. A. Smyth (RAMC), Captain L. D. Stone (RAMC) and Regimental Sergeant-Major Sandy McTavish (Argyll and Sutherland Highlanders). For each of them it was a welcome contact with a friendly face from the outside world for the first time in three and a half years. More importantly, it was confirmation that their ordeal – and that of the other Prisoners – was coming to an end at last. The meetings were all too brief, but requisitions for further supplies were taken and Major Smiley was able to explain why he had to remain undercover.

Sergeant Collins contacted HQ in Calcutta with the information obtained from the officers and on 28 August supplies, including newspapers, started to arrive by air. The RAPWI report of 28 August 1945 states that at *'Camp B6 Ubon'* the nominal roll was 1459 British, one hundred Australian, four Americans and 1437 miscellaneous. This included twenty seriously sick and 300 others sick. Otherwise health was good. This was a total of 3,000, different from the information originally received by Major Smiley, but this discrepancy was relatively unimportant as numbers often varied. For example, RAPWI Sit Rep 16 dated 11 September 1945 states there was a total of 3,032 POWs (1,462 British, 102 Australian, 1,468 Dutch, the four Americans having left the camp by this date).

The code word '*Goldfish*' was finally passed to all Force 136 officers on 28 August. Needless to say, Major Smiley and his fellow officers were relieved to come out of hiding and start their work. The first medical teams arrived by air that evening and in subsequent days there was a steady stream of aircraft bringing in much-needed supplies, including Red Cross stores, food, clothing and medical aid.

Nai Tiang had placed the Seri Thai guerrillas into strategic areas around the Ubon camp ready to assist with any requests for help from inside the camp. No official figures of the number of Seri Thai members involved at Ubon have survived but estimates suggest that 3,000 men came from the Ubon area alone. (John B Haseman in his book *The Thai Resistance Movement During WW2*, estimates that Seri Thai guerrillas at Sakhon Nakhon numbered 3,500, and at Udon Thani 1,200. Former Prisoner William Wilder sketched a portrait of Seri Thai partisan Nai Ouen Obichitta, who was from Nakhon Phanom.)

In the weeks before the end of the war, the Ubon Prisoners were unaware that a group of British officers were operating in the region, but there was a sense of change within the camp. Harold Churchill recalls that at the end of July 1945 an RAF bomber flew over the camp and dropped leaflets stating that the Allies had landed in Japan, captured Tokyo and the Emperor had fled the country. This was propaganda, of course, but nevertheless added to the Prisoners' growing optimism that the Allies had taken the upper hand.

Their newfound faith was short-lived when Major Chida detailed them to dig deep trenches across the airstrip. The Prisoners speculated this was to prevent Allied aircraft from landing. Rumours of an imminent end to the war filtered into the camp from local Thai villages, but a lack of interpretation led to dubious conclusions. Some men speculated that if the Japanese did lose the war, they would turn on the Prisoners to seek revenge. This fear had some credence; after the war, it was revealed that the Japanese high command had ordered that

143

Prisoners should be executed if the Allies invaded Thailand. The trenches dug across the airstrip were not intended to prevent Allied aircraft from landing but were mass graves for the Prisoners.

In the first week of August, the men noticed that the guards appeared less aggressive; the Prisoners' work became less urgent and on some days some men were not required to work at all. The dawn of 15 August 1945 was significant because it was three and a half years since the Fall of Singapore on 15 February 1942, the date when their imprisonment started. Charles Steel wrote in a letter to his wife that the Japanese organised sporting events on that day but cancelled them at the last minute. Maurice Naylor remembers that the working parties were assembled but there was a sense of confusion and panic as he witnessed Japanese guards destroying papers and records. William Wilder remembers he was given the day off and his dark mood noticeably improved as his optimism grew. Other working parties were told to clean equipment and put it into stores; there was to be no more work.

RSM McTavish was also aware of a change in atmosphere. He was ordered to go to Major Chida's office, where he was told that an 'atom bomb' had been dropped in Japan and the Japanese had surrendered. No one else in the camp knew officially that the war was over and there was no way that RSM McTavish could verify this news.

It was not until the evening of 18 August that Major Chida took to his raised platform in front of a full parade ground of Prisoners to make an announcement. He looked pale and drawn and was dressed in full uniform with his ceremonial sword at his side.

The parade listened intently to this diminutive man as he addressed the Prisoners in Japanese, which was translated into English. His speech was reproduced in the camp's newspaper, the *Newsphere*.

HIS OWN WORDS
MAJOR CHIDA ANNOUNCES END OF WAR
18th AUG 1945

The camp commandant wishes to say a few words.
The Greater East Asia war has ended.
You must carry on as you have been for some time until your own
people come and take you over.
I, as camp commandant, wish to thank you all for the good work
you have done under me in the group.
Higher officials have given out certain orders and it is my wish
that you adhere to these orders in a soldierly manner.
I am still responsible for you all until I can hand you over to your
own people. Outside work will cease as from tomorrow. Inside
work as far as the I.J.A. are concerned is also finished, but work
will have to carry on as before for your own benefit. Do your
work as exercise. Those of you who are fit must keep fit. Those
who are sick must do their utmost to get fit as soon as possible.

Major Chida was too uncomfortable to announce who had won and there was no mention of the word 'surrender', but his demeanour and shamefulness told the real story. At that moment nothing else mattered and the men looked at each other in disbelief; at last the war was over. After a few moments, someone started to sing the British national anthem. Everyone joined in the celebration as a wave of joy and emotion spread through the camp. The Dutch, the Australians and most likely the four Americans started singing and cheering as well. Many men were moved to tears of joy; others just stared in bewilderment. Fergus Anckorn remembered that '*at last I could say NO!*'.

In the days that followed, the Japanese and Korean guards remained in their camp; apart from an occasional patrol, there was little interaction between them and the men who were now free to enjoy their liberty. The men did not know what to do next but there must have been some apprehension of Japanese reprisals. They maintained admirable discipline and remained in the camp calmly talking and chatting amongst themselves.

In one incident a Japanese guard nicknamed 'Efficiency' vigorously shook the hand of one of the ex-Prisoners whilst he said, *'All finish, England and Nippon now OK.'* It was said that Efficiency was dressed in civilian clothes and smiling through his magnificent teeth. This was a total surprise because 'Efficiency' was a notorious sadist who had ill-treated many Prisoners, including during an incident on the journey between Bangkok and Ubon. He was clearly a coward looking for forgiveness; it is doubtful he received it.

Inevitably they had to wait for whatever was to come next, and they had to be patient. After a couple of days of waiting, wondering and hoping, an Allied aircraft flew overhead and dropped leaflets. There were four types: one intended for Allied Ex-Prisoners of War; one for Japanese prison guards; one for local Japanese forces, and the fourth for the local native population.

The leaflets for the ex-Prisoners announced the Allied victory, provided advice on eating, and assured them that help was on the way. This was part of Operation Birdcage, which was authorised to drop leaflets on all known POW camps, not just Ubon. It was intended to raise 'morale' amongst the men and was a precursor to Operation Mastiff, which was the provision of 'physical' relief by supplying, clothing, medicine and crucial personnel, such as medics.

The leaflet for ex-Prisoners is reproduced below from Lieutenant Cornelis B. Evers book *Death Railway.*

> *TO ALL ALLIED PRISONERS OF WAR*
> *THE JAPANESE FORCES HAVE*
> *SURRENDERED UNCONDITIONALLY*
> *AND THE WAR IS OVER*

We will get supplies to you as soon as it is humanly possible, and we will make arrangements to get you out. Because of the distance involved it may be some time before we can achieve this.

YOU will help us and yourselves if you act as follows:
Stay in your camp until you get further orders from us.
Start preparing nominal rolls of personnel giving the fullest particulars.
List your most urgent necessities.
If you have been starved or underfed for long periods do not eat large quantities of solid food, fruit or vegetables at first. It is dangerous for you to do so. Small quantities at frequent intervals are much safer and will strengthen you far more quickly.
For those who are really ill or very weak fluids such as broths and soups making use of the water in which rice and other foods have been boiled are much the best.
Gifts of food from the local populations should be cooked. We want to get you back home quickly, safe and sound, and we do not want you to risk diarrhoea, dysentery and cholera at this last stage.
Local authorities and or Allied officers will take charge of your affairs in a very short time. Be guided by their advice.

Rumours that the Americans had dropped something called an atom bomb on Japan spread throughout the camp. This new weapon was difficult for the men to comprehend as technology had moved on at quite a pace since February 1942. They asked themselves how could one bomb inflict so much damage and kill so many people and be so powerful that it brought a sudden end to the war?

The war officially ended on 2 September 1945, when Peace Treaties were signed on board USS *Missouri* anchored in Tokyo Bay. But all that mattered to the men in the Ubon camp was that at last they were going home and, as a big bonus, the Japanese were defeated.

The ex-Prisoners were unaware that the Japanese High Command previously instructed their POW camp commanders to prepare to execute Prisoners when and if the Allies invaded Thailand. There was no invasion and the orders were not given, but the men were instinctively nervous that upon surrender the Japanese guards might lose face and seek vengeance.

147

Hirohito accepted the terms of the Potsdam Declaration, which was agreed by the Allies on 26 July, before the Hiroshima atom bomb. It came with a warning that the Allies *'Will not deviate from them (the terms). There are no alternatives. We shall brook no delay'.* It ended with a final warning *'We call upon the government of Japan to proclaim now the unconditional surrender of all Japanese armed forces, and to provide proper and adequate assurances of their good faith in such action. The alternative for Japan is prompt and utter destruction.'*

With the realisation that atom bombs could lead to extensive loss of life and widespread damage, Hirohito and his advisors were well aware of the consequences if they failed to honour their acceptance of the Declaration. Nevertheless, there was an element of luck that local Japanese officers waited for orders not to execute the Prisoners and did not take matters into their own hands.

The Japanese at Ubon did not seek revenge or attempt to inflict further abuse on the men. They retained their weapons because there was no Allied officer senior enough to accept their surrender (Major Smiley was still undercover at this stage). The liberated men were allowed their freedom, but RSM McTavish appointed military policemen to keep a look out for trouble. However, there were no serious concerns and behaviour was generally good although boisterous on occasions. When problems did arise, it was usually blamed on local rice whiskey. The inebriated were taken back to the camp to sober up.

Initially the priority was to find a decent supply of food. Small groups were organised to go to the Ubon markets. The governor of Ubon, Luang Narat Raksa, who was also a Seri Thai partisan, was a very generous man; on behalf of the people of Ubon, he provided the camp with fresh food and livestock without charge. Despite the leaflets advising the men to eat little and often, many chose to eat as much as they could!

Many of the men at Ubon had at some point been under the command of Colonel Phillip Toosey. He was an officer in the 135th Field Regiment Royal Artillery and senior officer in several camps, most notably at Tarmarkan, the camp close to the famous Bridge on the River Kwai. Colonel Toosey was a remarkable man who earned total respect from his men by defending them from the Japanese. In return he demanded their discipline and good behaviour.

He was being held at the officers' camp Nakhon Nayok when the Japanese surrendered. His thoughts immediately turned to his men at the Ubon camp. On 22 August he moved to Bangkok with the intention to travel to Ubon, but it would take some time to arrange transport. Whilst he was waiting, a British civilian internee called Peter Heath took the trouble to find Colonel Toosey and invited him to dine at a Bangkok restaurant.

Peter Heath had been held in a civilian internment camp run by the Royal Thai Army. It was said that the conditions there were much less harsh than in any other Japanese camp. Peter was involved in what was known as the 'V Scheme'. Considerable amounts of money were raised by the internees and smuggled into prison camps in the Nong Pladuk area. The Prisoners used the money to buy extra food and much-needed medical supplies from the local Thai people. The scheme probably saved many lives.

Colonel Toosey did not meet Peter whilst the scheme was running, but he was extremely grateful to all those who took huge personal risks to help the Prisoners. At the restaurant, Colonel Toosey was delighted to meet another important associate of the V Scheme, Boon Pong. At considerable risk to his own life, he had smuggled large amounts of money hidden in baskets of food into the camps. It was a welcome opportunity for Colonel Toosey to thank Boon Pong personally for his heroic efforts.

A few weeks later, Boon Pong was severely wounded in a shooting incident and British doctors were called upon to save his life. After the war he started a bus company but unfortunately ran into financial difficulties. Back in England, Colonel Toosey and other officers involved in the V Scheme learned of his predicament and raised £38,000 to enable him to regenerate his business.

Two days after the meeting, Peter Heath persuaded the Thai authorities to provide a train for Colonel Toosey and his officers to travel to Ubon. The Japanese objected but they now had to get used to being over-ruled; on 25 August, a party of thirty officers set off in high spirits for Ubon. They had the comfort of a coach with wooden seats, which was a far cry from the fetid cattle wagons in which they had endured the tortuous journey from Singapore three and a half years earlier. But the train was just as slow.

In the late afternoon of the next day they arrived in Ubon at Warin Chamrap station. News that a contingent of British officers was on its way had been telegraphed ahead. The governor organised and presided over the official welcoming party, which included the Royal Thai Army commander and other local officials and dignitaries who impressed each other with their smart uniforms. In stark contrast, Colonel Toosey and his party disembarked from the train still wearing threadbare uniforms that were now almost four years old.

After the obligatory greetings and handshakes, the officers were driven to the ferry where they were greeted by a resplendent British soldier dressed in full uniform. He had borrowed various components from several men in the camp. It was perhaps the only complete British army uniform in the whole of Ubon; although surprised, Colonel Toosey was touched by its significance. The soldier, whose name may never be known, was an emotional symbol of the honour, pride and discipline instilled in Colonel Toosey's men who, despite their despair, disenchantment and the disgraceful treatment to which they had been subjected, had survived with their dignity totally intact. It was a very significant moment and together they led the convoy to the camp where the remainder of the ex-Prisoners were waiting patiently.

It was early evening when the officers arrived at the camp to a rapturous welcome. Reports previously received by Colonel Toosey about the Ubon camp had given him the impression that conditions were poor and he had fears of men starving and sick, but when he saw them his concerns were put aside. The men were in good shape and only twenty were in the hospital. Their main privation was a lack of suitable clothing, which made the resplendent soldier at the railway station all the more remarkable.

One of the officers in the party, Louis Baume, wrote in his diary that *'Our reception on arrival was terrific. That they were genuinely overjoyed to see us was obvious – they seemed as happy to see us as we were to see them.'*

In his report, Colonel Toosey made a special note that the camp had been run smoothly and incidents with the Japanese were comparatively rare. He noted the shootings of Robert Merritt and Salomon Abas. There was a special note that RSM McTavish and WOI Slotboom had fulfilled their duties in a *'splendid manner'*.

No doubt the re-union celebrations lasted well into the night, with good food and possibly alcohol of some sort in ample quantities. Ubon's governor, Luang Narat Raksa, generously provided everything for the party.

The following day, Monday 27 August 1945, Major Smiley, having received the *'Goldfish'* code word, arrived in the camp and met Colonel Toosey for the first time. Colonel Toosey reported that Major Smiley was accompanied by Major Hudson, Major Blaithwaite and American OSS officer Major Griswald. (Note that record HS1 326 in the National Archives at Kew, states the *'Goldfish'* code word was broadcast to SOE officers on 28 August. The date 27 August above is quoted from Major Hudson's operational report.)

Shortly after the arrival of the SOE officers, all ex-Prisoners were called onto the parade ground. Colonel Toosey invited Major Smiley to speak to them, presumably about their liberation and what he was doing to secure their departure. He then inspected the men, regularly stopping to speak to individuals.

Colonel Toosey later wrote that the parade was '*a most inspiring sight to see these splendid men together with their discipline still intact after three and a half years of absolute hell and I was extremely proud of them.*' Major Smiley recalled in his memoir that he was struck by the makeshift clothes the men were wearing: hats made of straw, tattered shorts or 'ball bags', and either bare feet or home-made clogs. It was a harrowing sight but the men were proud and erect as the Japanese flag was replaced by the Union Jack, which had been concealed throughout the incarceration. The emotion was overwhelming as they sang the National Anthem, and even the battle-hardened Major Smiley had difficulty holding back tears. The camp was officially liberated.

After the parade, the men surrounded Major Smiley, Colonel Toosey and the officers. They were eager to ask for the latest – and not so latest – news about the war. They were desperate to know when they would receive letters from their families and when they would be returning home. Later that evening Major Smiley appeared on the theatre stage and answered many more questions in a gathering that lasted for two hours.

Charles Steel hosted a meal for some of the officers and came away with the expectation that the journey home would begin within fourteen days. Unfortunately, it took much longer.

After speaking to the men Major Smiley had a serious meeting with Major Chida to discuss the transfer of command and other issues. In the confines of his office, Major Chida confessed that he and his men had helped themselves to Red Cross parcels addressed to the Prisoners. Evidence of this injustice was clear as he had made no effort to conceal the packets of State Express cigarettes on his desk, which the Red Cross regularly included in their welfare parcels. He also revealed that the Japanese had helped themselves to life-saving medical supplies and other items from the parcels. He confessed to Major Smiley, who was now enraged, that letters addressed to Prisoners were routinely withheld and stored in a separate room within the camp.

On the 30 August, Captain James White of the 16 Parachute Battalion and Captain Lang of 'A' Force, together with two others, were parachuted into Ubon. They were brought in by Liberator and dropped in the area at night. Captain White approached the camp in the open and let the Japanese guards see him throw his rifle to the ground. Then he walked towards the main gate with one of his men. The guards put down their rifles and escorted them to Colonel Toosey.

Colonel Toosey, assisted by Major Reggie Lees and Regimental Sergeant Major McTavish, took over the running of the camp from Major Chida. They arranged entertainment to keep the men occupied and useful work to keep the camp clean and pleasant. Major Smiley moved his HQ to the police buildings near to Ubon's aerodrome where Sergeant Collins set up his radio and maintained daily contact HQ in Calcutta.

The first few Liberators dropped supplies at the camp, but several parachutes caused damage to the huts and were an obvious danger to the men. The drop zone was changed to the aerodrome. Supplies were provided by aircraft operating under Operation Mastiff, and Ubon, because of its remoteness, had high priority. The liberated men collected the supplies, loaded the trucks and drove back to the camp. There was disbelief when they found cases of tins of rice; it was the last food they wanted after surviving on little else for the last three and a half years! There was also a delivery of a new drug called penicillin. None of the medical staff had heard of this and did not know how it should be administered. A medic was sent from HQ to show them how to use this new wonder drug.

Colonel Toosey realised that, with their freedom and improving general condition, some of the men might be tempted to seek out the company of Ubon's beautiful young ladies. He knew that, when one thing led to another, there was a likelihood that an intimate amorous encounter would inevitably follow. He did not want to stop the men from their romantic adventures, but he had a duty to remind them of the possible serious medical consequences that might result from such passionate engagements. Ever the man to find a practical solution, he ordered condoms from HQ. Next day a consignment of 10,000 arrived! HQ were amazed at the potency of the ex-Prisoners, but Colonel Toosey was equally surprised that HQ could deliver such a large quantity at short notice!

Now that the men had the wherewithal to avoid catching an unwanted and embarrassing infection, there arose the delicate issue of arranging discreet liaisons between Ubon's ladies and the men who wished to end their enforced celibacy and check if they had retained the power with which to perform. Whilst it is true to say that most of Ubon's ladies had very strict principles and did not generally behave in a promiscuous way, there were some whose disposition inevitably led them to profit from a brief lustful entanglement or two.

Major Smiley, with the help of Ubon's Chief of Police, organised a series of brothels. There were several rooms for the ex-Prisoners and one room for the exclusive use of the officers, which they called the 'Chinese Hotel'. This ensured that outbreaks of trouble were prevented, or at least contained, and the ladies were kept safe. One problem was that none of the men had disposable income with which to pay for the services they desired. Upon realising that this would be an awkward and demeaning situation, the enterprising Major Smiley introduced a special form which the men had to sign in the boudoir; and the ladies were subsequently required to present this to his office to claim payment for their service. The standard rate for a brief rendezvous was three panels of parachute silk. The ladies and Major Smiley readily agreed with this arrangement because the value of parachute silk on the black market was about £1 per panel. Major Smiley reckoned that the ladies knew that parachutes had a greater value and that they also knew how to convert the panels to make more money! He also knew how to save money.

However, it was distressing to learn that the Japanese had brought comfort girls to Ubon. Hundreds of thousands unfortunate young women and girls from Japanese occupied countries were deceived with promises of legitimate work that paid good money. They left their families and homelands behind and were thrust into sexual slavery in Japanese military brothels in camps throughout South East Asia. Tragically, a small group of at least fifteen Korean girls were sent to Ubon. After the surrender, they came to Major Smiley pleading that they were being held against their will. It transpired that the Japanese claimed they were holding them because they had been paid for services they had not provided. Major Smiley declared the debt null and void and ordered the immediate release of all the girls. He found appropriate safe accommodation for them, where they were guarded by the police.

The governor of Ubon organised entertainment to keep the men occupied. A popular event was horse racing held every weekend in Ubon's central recreation area of Thung Si Muang. The small ponies were ridden by even smaller young boys around a short course. There were several races at each meet and extra interest was provided by a popular betting shop. It is not known how much money the men had with which to place bets, but nevertheless it was a very enjoyable way to pass the time.

Further entertainment was provided by troupes of dancers from the surrounding villages who came to the camp to give performances of traditional Thai dancing. Since the early 1700s there was little change in the format and symbolism of these dances. Dancing and music were great social activities, as well as being an essential part of all celebrations and anniversaries. The dances told stories, often of boy chasing a girl or depicting work in the rice fields. The music was provided by drums of various sizes and tones, cymbals (often made out of coconut shells or bamboo), and a *khan*, an instrument made out of hollowed bamboo similar in appearance to pan pipes and played in the same way. The performances were much appreciated by the men. The camp's newsletter, the *Newsphere*, reported that '*while the performance was new and strange to most of the audience, one and all agreed on the intense rhythm running through the show'.*

The concert party also provided wonderful entertainment and a performance was hastily arranged for the 20 August. It was called the Victory Show and arguably most enjoyable because it celebrated the immense euphoria and relief of their freedom. A 'V' for victory was painted on the front curtain. The incredibly ambitious show included a mock American bomber aircraft with rotating propellers that was lowered onto the stage with actors waving out of its windows. The show was a huge hit and included a victory song, specially written by ex-Prisoner Bob Gale.

Out of the blue came freedom,
The freedom that we've all been waiting for,
Out of the blue came freedom,
The freedom that we know we all adore.
We're gonna start to build a new world,
A world of peace we've all been waiting for.
So thank you Uncle Joe, John Bull and Uncle Sam,
For bringing us our freedom once more.

In the first edition of the *Newsphere*, ex-Prisoner CQS Ray Fairclough complimented a production called *Escapado Argentina,* written and produced by Bob Gale. The orchestra was led by Nico Bruns with a choir consisting of Dutch ex-Prisoners.

Silent movies were shown at Ubon's cinema. There was always confusion and hilarity amongst the audience as the projectionist mixed up the film reels so that the end of the movie was often seen before the beginning and the performance could start with the middle reel; more often than not, the projector broke down.

The people of Ubon responded marvellously, especially those living close to the camp. The governor encouraged them to organise parties and picnics and to invite the men into their homes. Even though conversation was difficult due to language differences, there was plenty of good-humoured charades and sign language.

156

Young children living around the camp were encouraged to meet and talk to the men. Khun Thongdee Wongman was twelve years old when the camp was liberated. In 2019, he clearly remembered his parents inviting groups of ex-Prisoners into his home to talk, eat and pass the time. Dutch ex-Prisoner M. Soesman wrote that the reception received by the men from the people of Ubon was very cordial and most welcome.

Unfortunately, on some occasions as the wait to go home lengthened frustration led to trouble. Isolated incidents of drunkenness, breaking into property and petty crime were reported to the Chief of Police. Major Smiley appointed Captain Tom Phillips of the Norfolk Regiment as unofficial 'town mayor', with orders to snuff out any trouble as soon as it occurred. If issues were reported to the police, Major Smiley acted as mediator to make amends.

The editorial in the second issue of *Newsphere* reminded its readers that Colonel Toosey trusted the men to go outside the camp into Ubon, but officially this was contrary to general orders. It reminded the men that the colonel had put his faith and trust in them to behave appropriately, and this privilege could be easily withdrawn. The editorial described the people of Ubon as friendly, generous, welcoming and proud of their heritage, and told the men to show respect to their hosts' customs and traditions. Unfortunately five men were reported to have betrayed Colonel Toosey's trust, and their behaviour jeopardised the continuation of the privilege. The men are not named, neither is the decision to withdraw the privilege reported.

Some of the men organised their own sporting events, including cricket matches between the British and the Australians, athletics events and football matches. At least one football match was played between the British and a side from Ubon. The *Newsphere* reported that there was a large crowd on the parade ground, including several ladies as guests of the governor's wife who caught the eyes of the team and spectators. By half-time the British, led by Captain Boyle, were winning by three goals scored by Gunner Dodd and two from Private Graves. In the second half Captain Blesser scored a fourth goal for the British side, and Ubon scored a consolation goal past goalkeeper Lieutenant Primrose.

The Allied officers spent many evenings at parties hosted by one or other of Ubon's dignitaries. The hospitality provided to them was typical of Thai friendliness and generosity, and given freely in honour to their guests. The officers reciprocated by holding similar parties and meals inside the camp. Each occasion was followed by lavish entertainment, sometimes provided by the camp's theatre group. On 3 September there was special reason to celebrate: Major Smiley's promotion to Lieutenant-Colonel, and Nai Tiang Sirikhandra and Nai Chamlong Daorueang ministerial appointments into the new Thai government.

Whilst it isn't possible to verify every party, Major Peter Kemp recalls that most of the ones in north-east Thailand followed a typical pattern, which was never tiresome. On one occasion, a local village held a party to celebrate Major Kemp's birthday. He described long tables laden with roast suckling pig, ducks, chickens, vegetables and huge tureens of rice. On other tables there were earthenware jars, called *changs*, each containing a thick layer of rice floating on top of a slightly sweet but potent beer. Each *chang* had several straws and was shared between guests.

The major was amazed that such a feast could be mustered in a small, rain-soaked village in the middle of the tropics. At most parties the guests helped themselves to the copious quantities of Issan regional delicacies such as snails, frogs, ant eggs, bamboo, all accompanied by very hot chilli sauces. Also available was *lao kao* whisky made from fermented rice; extremely powerful, it often had a devasting effect.

After the food, the entertainment began with traditional Issan music called *molam*. Drums and *khans* accompanied the nasal-sounding singing of traditional folk songs handed down through the generations. Then it was the turn of the honoured guests to sing their favourite song in a 1940s' style karaoke. By this time the guests were often drunk and willingly put any inhibitions to one side, with predictable results. At his birthday party, Major Kemp sang the Polish revolutionary song *Warszawiaka* with sublime alcoholic exuberance. It was met with polite, if somewhat bewildered, applause from the hosts and laughter from his friends and other foreign guests.

After the singing came the dancing. The slender and elegant figures of the Thai dancers moved gracefully around the room, but, when the inebriated guests were invited to join in, the exquisite display degenerated into drunken despair. Next morning, when nursing serious hangovers, the previous night's excesses were greeted with good humour from the Thais, a sure sign that the party had been a great success.

Some generous people from Ubon provided a radio, which was placed in the canteen for all to hear. At evening mealtimes it was tuned into a special BBC broadcast from Delhi intended for all released Prisoners in South East Asia. Some of the men decided to write articles from the broadcast for the *Newsphere*. In an article reported in the 28 September 1945 edition of the *Sevenoaks Chronicle*, Fergus Anckorn was reported to be at least one of the men who took notes in shorthand.

The *Newsphere* newsletter was produced by a team calling themselves the New Freedom Co-operators, and their company was the General Release Company at No 1 Group Camp, Ubon. The editor was pre-war journalist Colin Hubbard. Three editions of *Newsphere* were produced during the six weeks wait for repatriation. Each edition presented news and reports from Great Britain, with stories about memories of what life was like back home and what might have changed. There were light-hearted articles peppered with banter and leg pulling. Illustrations and cartoons were expertly drawn by Dutch artist Jan Van de Holthe.

Somehow, Colin and his 'press office' team were able to access a printing press to reproduce the newsletter. This may have been the Roneo printing machine supplied to Nai Tiang when Force

136 made initial contact. It is also possible that the press office may have had access to printing presses in Ubon; either way, the *Newsphere* was a great distraction for the men as they waited to leave for home. Only four copies of each edition were printed but at least one copy was put in a folder and passed around the camp for the men to read.

The first issue, dated Saturday 1 September 1945, contained twelve pages with articles taken from the radio broadcasts, stories about interesting escapades in the camps, politics and opinions on the outcome of the war. It included reviews of the latest films and film stars, musicians and entertainers, and a show produced by the camp concert party. There was a report on the VE Day celebrations in London, sports news, and chess and bridge puzzles. On page three there was a fitting tribute to Colonel Toosey and his officers. On page seven there was a cartoon of Major Chida and the transcript of his speech announcing the end of the war. Also, there was a story about how a secret radio belonging to a British officer was smuggled out of Kanburi camp in a mattress belonging to a Japanese officer and successfully found its way into the camp at Nakhon Nayok.

The second issue was published only four days later, on 5 September. It contained a short article and tribute to the activities of Major Smiley and the local Seri Thai. Other pages reported football, cricket and athletics news, including an account of the race over one mile between Sydney Wooderson and the Swede Arne Andersson at White City on August Bank holiday (1945). There were several articles remembering life in Britain, including articles on holidays, fashion and theatre based on pre-war memories and notes taken from the BBC broadcasts.

After years of privation, the men were thinking more about home each day. The *Newsphere* helped them, but for some their expectations were very different to the realities they eventually met.

The third edition was released on 8 September 1945. Its front cover was headlined *Back to Work* and the imagination of Van de Holthe produced a cartoon drawing of two couples cavorting in the office in a manner that would not be considered politically correct in the twenty-first century. Inside there were more serious articles about politics, the workings of the atomic bomb, and a medical report by Major Smyth analysing hospital admissions between June 1942 and August 1945. There was a review of books and films and an article on the future of the motorcycle.

Religion continued to play an important role in the camp after the liberation. Padre Ross found his work much easier when he could write more optimistic sermons than those of the previous three-and-a-half years. Thanksgiving services were popular and frequently left the padre in demand. In the third issue of *Newsphere,* he wrote that the question he was most asked was 'When are we going home?' He admitted he did not know, but went on to say that he would be very disappointed if they were not back by Christmas. He whetted the appetite for Christmas with anticipation of Christmas puddings and the warmth of home and family.

In his final report, Colonel Toosey remarked that the Royal Thai Army provided extra food free of charge. The Thai authorities were very generous, and he was complimentary about the facilities provided for the ex-Prisoners whilst they waited for orders to repatriate. He wrote: *'Everybody in this camp (Ubon) will remember with great pleasure the kindness and generosity shown to us by the people of Ubon.'*

When Major Smiley moved from the Royal Thai Army base to the police buildings near the aerodrome, he was delighted that three ex-Prisoners volunteered to help him. Sergeant R. M. Neave (2nd Battalion, The Gordon Highlanders) helped Sergeant Collins with radio cypher work and Major Smiley with a mountain of administration. Lance Corporal J. A. Phillips (Royal Army Service Corps) was Major Smiley's driver and mechanic who ensured that personnel cars and other vehicles previously owned by the Japanese were available at all times. He had a wicked sense of humour, which he still retained despite three-and-a-half years of imprisonment. Sergeant G. H. Thomas

(Royal Army Ordnance Corps) could speak Japanese fluently and became Major Smiley's interpreter.

Throughout his time as a Prisoner, Sergeant Thomas had acted as camp interpreter on behalf of RSM McTavish. This often resulted in unjustified beatings and humiliation following the complaints and messages he was obliged to present to the Japanese commanders and guards. His mother was Japanese, which may have made him a target for further unjustified brutality.

It was remarkable that each of these men volunteered to stay behind with Major Smiley after the rest of the ex-Prisoners had left the camp. They quickly became part of the team and enjoyed the happy-go-lucky ambience which was characteristic of Major Smiley's style of leadership and discipline.

Chapter 16

GOING HOME – AT LAST

Most of the Dutch ex-Prisoners in Thailand came from the Dutch East Indies. After the war finished, there was a nationalist uprising in their homeland, which was hostile to the prospect of returning to a Dutch colony. It was considered too dangerous for the recently liberated Dutch ex-Prisoners to return. This was disturbing and depressing news especially as the British and Australians eagerly looked forward to their own imminent departure.

Colonel Toosey and his team worked with various agencies, including RAPWI (Repatriation of Allied Prisoners of War and Internees), to organise the repatriation of the ex-Prisoners. There were twenty men in poor health when Colonel Toosey arrived at the camp and he instructed they were to be put on the next available train to Bangkok, where they would receive better treatment in more comfortable hospitals with appropriate facilities and medicines. He advised the four Americans to travel with them so that they could join up with other American ex-Prisoners who were being assembled at Bangkok's godown district by their own repatriation teams. This was the same location in which they were held on their journey to Ubon just six months earlier.

The sick and the Americans left Ubon on 28 August on a wood-fired steam train that pulled coaches fitted with cushioned seats, an absolute comfort for them. It made regular stops to replenish its fuel and to refill the water tanks. Whenever they pulled into a siding, local Thai people surrounded the train hoping to catch a glimpse of the men. Many of them gave gifts of food and drink. At one stop, the Americans were each given a small parcel containing shaving cream, soap, toothbrush and toothpaste. It was the first time in three-and-a-half years that they had cleaned their teeth properly.

In Bangkok the Americans were driven to the godowns but, when they arrived, they learned that there were available seats on an aircraft that was about to depart for Rangoon from Don Muang Airport. None of them waited. In no time at all they were in Rangoon, eating their favourite American food before departing to Calcutta.

Within days of the camp's liberation Major Smiley instructed the Japanese to prepare Ubon's operational airstrip for the evacuation of the ex-Prisoners. But after two weeks there was growing impatience amongst the men that the authorities in Bangkok were taking too long to arrange their repatriation. Colonel Toosey decided to take action and travelled back to Bangkok by light aircraft in an attempt to expedite the process for the British and Australians. Despite his efforts to secure a plan with RAPWI, however, there was still no immediate prospect of the men leaving Ubon.

Some liberated men from other camps in Thailand arriving in Bangkok had to wait several days for a flight to Rangoon where they would board a ship to return the British Isles. The temptations of the lively post-war Thai capital were too hard to resist for some of them. Discipline was hard to enforce, so the authorities decided that the troublemakers should be sent home as a priority to avoid further disquiet. The men in Ubon were at an unfair disadvantage because of their good behaviour and, because Ubon was remote, they had to wait as other ex-Prisoners nearer to the concentration centre at Bangkok were prioritised. A RAPWI situation report dated 10 September revealed the men were still waiting for instructions.

On 20 September the authorities in Bangkok finally decided it was impractical to evacuate the men from Ubon by air and instead they would travel to Bangkok by train. It seems an obvious decision; aircraft were in high demand in Thailand and consequently there was an acute shortage, especially the number required to complete the fifty or so missions needed to accommodate 1,600 men on aircraft that could only safely carry about thirty men at a time.

Now that they had received the green light, 101 Australians under the command of Major Ewart and 250 British left the camp on 22 September for the railway station at Warin Chamrap, where they boarded a train on the first leg of their journey home. In his memoirs, Major Smiley admits the Australians' behaviour had caused problems with the Thai authorities, which he had to resolve, and he writes that he was *'very relieved'* when they departed.

They had to cross the river Mun by sampan but the river was now running high, fast and wide following the monsoon rainfall. It took forty-five minutes for a sampan loaded with five or six men to travel across. This was a huge problem for a relatively small batch of men; it was going to be an even greater issue for the 1,200 British due to cross the river two days later.

The Royal Thai Army 9th Infantry Regiment hosted a farewell party for the remaining British men on the eve of their departure. On 24 September, the bleary-eyed ex-Prisoners patiently lined up in the camp to climb aboard Japanese lorries for the seven-mile drive to the river crossing. Major Chida had already been sent to Singapore to stand trial for the war crimes he was accused of committing in previous camps, but most of his men stood at the gate and saluted each lorry as it passed by. This gesture made Louis Baume feel pity for the Japanese, and the absent Major Chida in particular, but at the same time he held them in contempt for their actions and behaviour towards him and his fellow ex-Prisoners.

The river crossing took eight hours to complete and it was 5pm before the last group crossed the river. They stayed at the Royal Thai Army barracks that night and boarded the train next morning. There is no surviving evidence but it can be imagined that the Royal Thai Army and the Ubon public turned out to give them a memorable send-off, such is the warm and affectionate nature of Ubon people. There would have been dancing, singing and colourful displays of flowers amongst the chaos of temporary food stalls selling everything from fried bananas to meat balls.

The men were crowded into passenger carriages, which were very different from the steel wagons in which they had travelled before. John Sartin wrote to his parents that every station was lined with Thai people handing them gifts of fruit, flowers and food. It was in stark contrast to their journey to Ubon earlier in the year when the Thais lined the platforms but stood in silence, fearing that to approach the men would result in shots being fired by the Japanese guards.

The train stopped at Korat, where they spent the night. The next morning, the ex-Prisoners set off for their final destination of Bangkok. John recalled that it was most convenient that the train stopped at Don Muang Airport next to the British concentration centre, where a few days later they were to board a flight to Rangoon. They were greeted by one of Lady Mountbatten's ladies in waiting.

Most of the men stayed for one or two nights before being flown in a Dakota aircraft to the central reception area at Rangoon. John wrote that about twenty-five men were assigned to each Dakota and two-and-a-half hours later they landed at Rangoon, having passed over the railway they built.

At Rangoon they received any necessary medical treatment and gradually regained fitness for the long voyage back to the British Isles. Some men had to stay in hospital for a lengthy period, among them Frank Sheppard who was hospitalised for two weeks. However, during this time he received mail from his family and was able to reply, informing them he was safe and on his way home.

The first port of call was usually Columbo where they re-stocked. They then sailed through the Suez Canal to Port Said, where some of the men spent a few days on dry land and were kitted out in fresh clothing to face the cold British climate. After passing through the Mediterranean and calling at Gibraltar for more supplies, they arrived in England to dreary November weather – but they were home and that was all that mattered to them.

The Australians left Bangkok and called at Singapore to pick up more men before setting sail for various ports in Australia. One such troopship was the *Highland Chieftain*.

Letters from Ubon

QMS J.E.Gilbert RAOC sent a letter from Ubon to his wife in Chelmsford on 5 September: '*Faring pretty well and being well looked after (at Ubon) and just bursting to get on the homeward journey. It is such a long time since we had contact with anybody civilised that I am afraid you cannot imagine how we shall feel when we do meet our dear ones again. The local authorities are helping as much as possible, getting us used to freedom, for which we have to thank God and our comrades who have fought to give it to us.*' QMS Gilbert was admitted to Ubon hospital on 27 June 1945 with bronchitis where he stayed for six days.

Gunner Fergus Anckorn sent a letter from Ubon in August 1945 to his parents in Sevenoaks: '*We are getting used to the feeling that it is all over. We now have a wireless and I listened to the news and good old Big Ben. The Thais have been marvellous to us, now they cannot do enough for us. We are in the finest camp and in fine fettle. Yours truly went in for a sports day yesterday – the first since home – and got a presentation for the 440 yards from the Governor of the locality, and I jumped 4ft 5ins in height, which is good for us. Our camp commandant is the best in Thailand and has stood up for our rights through thick and thin. He is Colonel Toosey – a fine man. I am feeling as fit as ever and ready for anything.* (Abridged)
The keystone to my good luck as a Prisoner of war has been my conjuring. If I had not been able to do that to entertain everybody I might not be here now. Things are much better here now, as we have had periodicals and newspapers dropped, and so beginning to find out all the things that have gone on in the past three and a half years.

167

We had never heard of jet-propelled aircraft. People here have sold everything they possess to get money: watches, pens, rings – even the gold in their teeth.

Here in camp I am the man who listens to London and India daily to take the news down in shorthand for the camp news sheet. Jolly good show! Last night I took down the news verbatim in shorthand, which was given out in French.'

Major Robinson Sherwood Foresters travelled with Colonel Toosey to Ubon camp from where he sent this letter: '*I have spent the last two days visiting "other ranks" camps with another colonel's party at Ubon. We had a wonderful reception all along the line by the Thais and a great reception by the troops. Later I returned in charge of twenty sick, the only bad cases out of 3,000 to the Thai Red Cross hospital at Bangkok.*

I spent one night at the Orient Hotel and I am now on my way back to Ubon. It has been wonderful to see our men again.

The conduct of the other ranks all through, even when they were living in conditions not fit for wild animals, has been wonderful. Their great spirit has sustained them, and that spirit was never broken. I can pay no tribute too high.'

Gunner Driver G. T. W. Ashcroft 88th Field Regiment Royal Artillery wrote to his parents in Preston of his hopes to be home for his 27th birthday. (Gunner Ashcroft's brother John was in the Royal Army Ordnance Corps but drowned in the sinking of HMT *Lancastria*. This was the biggest maritime disaster in British history, with estimates of fatalities varying between 3,000 and 5,800. The ship was bombed by German aircraft off the coast of St Nazaire on 17 June 1940, just two weeks after the Dunkirk evacuation.)

Private Douglas Purchase RAOC sent a letter to his parents in Sherbourne saying he was getting fit for the journey home. He wrote of the concerts and sports in the camp and his expectation that he would be home before Christmas. Private Purchase was admitted into Ubon hospital in April 1945 with an ulcer and detained for two-and-a-half weeks

Private Len Knott RAMC sent a letter to his future wife Joan on 13 September 1945. He described Ubon as *'this frightful dump'*. He complained that the tumultuous feeling that the war had finished was leaving him as his time at Ubon lengthened. He comments that he will have to get used to the everyday things he took for granted before the war, such as newspapers, soap, socks and bread. He says he will not return to his pre-war job because *'the monotony will drive me crackers'*. Neither was he looking forward to the English winter after six years of sunshine.

Len remarked on the generosity of the Thai people and was saddened that they had had to endure so much bomb damage in Bangkok. But the homeward train journey to Bangkok was *'hilarious travel, waving cheering Thais, boisterous boozy troops looking like nothing on earth with their ill-fitting clothes and bald nuts'*. He was *'revelling in the comfort of civilisation'*. He had missed Joan so much whilst in captivity, and was certain that thinking of her every day had pulled him through his terrible ordeal. Life on board ship passed by with little incident. He occupied his time by *'potter(ing) about, reading, sleeping, drinking tea, watching the sea and thinking of you (Joan)'*.

In a letter written on 14 October 1945 from the SS *Chitral*, Len was almost home but thinking back to the mental difficulties he had faced whilst in captivity: *'It was all too distant and impossible until I had to remind myself of sanity, and the very depths of hopelessness and despair forced me to resurrect these things and instil into myself the hope of better things, of being free, of the English countryside and you with your love and sweetness to me.'*

In the same letter his thoughts turned to how the last three-and-a-half years might have changed him: *'It's finished now, and we've had our quota of misery (I remember Marlowe saying once that he'd have a leg off if they'd send him home) and repression. I used to think that when I was free again I'd burst myself with frantic endeavour to catch the last delights of 3½ years, hardly stop to breathe, to defeat the insidious onset of time, but I now see that it's those very years which have taught me to stop, to go easy, to breathe steadily.'*

Len arrived in Southampton on 23 October 1945 and married Joan five months later in March 1946. They were together for fifty years until they sadly died within six weeks of each other in 1997.

Basil Fogg Royal Army Service Corps wrote a letter which was published in the *Kalgoorlie Miner* on 19 February 1947. He was searching for Ubon ex-Prisoners Ned Monte and Tubby Allen. Basil wrote that Ned and Tubby *'were the best pals a man ever had, and I can never forget their friendship nor the many kindnesses they showed me when the going was particularly tough.'* He wanted to thank them for their help. It is not known if he found his pals.

Private Leslie Knight RAOC wrote an account of his experience as a Prisoner of war for the *Worthing Gazette*. After being captured in Singapore in February 1942, he was imprisoned at Changi but transferred to the Roberts Hospital after a couple of months and was put on orderly duties in the dysentery wards. Shortly after this move, he was transferred with 600 hospital personnel to Kanburi in Thailand, where they built a base hospital for the railway. Leslie described conditions in the hospital as terrible: doctors had to use spoons, bits of wire and handsaws as surgical instruments. In December 1943 he moved to Nong Pladuk. It was here that Tom Brown, who was also from Worthing, recognised him. In an interview in January 2019, Tom recalled that he was in the hospital recovering from a bout of malaria when he thought he recognised the orderly carrying water through the hut. He asked him if he came from Worthing and Les replied that he did. They got talking and became great friends throughout the remainder of their captivity and on the way home. Tom said Les was built like a gorilla.

Leslie remembered that he did not sleep on the night when he heard that the war was over. He arrived in Worthing on 9 November and was greeted by his wife and his three-and-a-half-year-old son, whom he met for the first time.

PART 4

POST-LIBERATION IN UBON
AND NORTH-EAST THAILAND

Chapter 17

REMAINING TASKS AND DUTIES

The departure of the British, Australian and American troops did not signal the end of activity in Ubon. There were several 'loose ends' to finalise. The Dutch ex-Prisoners had to remain patient for their repatriation instructions because the nationalist uprising in the Dutch East Indies was still causing concern. There was also the matter of concentrating the Japanese soldiers from the region into Ubon, dis-arming them and preparing for their repatriation. In addition, there were reports of nationalist groups holding French internees against their will in small towns across the Mekong in French Indochina. It was a hostile situation and the SOE were required to assist before they could leave the area. Finally, Ubon required help to return to its pre-Japanese state of peace and quiet. There was much to do.

The Dutch

The Ubon camp was considered to be less brutal than camps in the west. Nevertheless, reports surfaced that some of the Dutch Prisoners were brutally treated by the Japanese in various incidents at the airstrip and Ubon aerodrome. Lodewyk Jan Weygers wrote of savage beatings and torturous punishments over minor transgressions. He recalls witnessing some of his fellow Prisoners being ordered to take up the push-up position over hot coals with dog excrement placed under their noses.

This particular incident took place at Ubon's smaller camp, which the Dutch referred to as Zenzietai. Four hundred Dutch Prisoners appear to have started work here from March 1945. The guards were an isolated group, most likely under the command of a particularly brutal officer, and they treated the Prisoners with considerably more ferocity than at the larger camp.

After the Japanese surrendered, Major Smiley ordered the guards from Zenzietai onto the parade ground and invited the Dutch ex-Prisoners to identify the Japanese miscreants. The offenders named by Lodewyk Jan Weygers were Bowleg, Goldtooth, Flag SOB, Gas SOB, Mussolini, Dracula, Animal Abuser, Ballpuller and Efficiency. They were all held in Ubon's prison cells until 6 October when they, plus two more unidentified guards, were sent by rail to Bangkok's infamous Bang Kwang jail before being sent to trial at the War Crimes court at Singapore. Bang Kwang jail is still open today, and is noted as one of the most feared jails in the world. It is referred to as the 'Bangkok Hilton'.

Because it was not considered safe to send the Dutch back to their homeland, they had to remain in the camp. They were no doubt despondent, homesick and understandably angry as the other Prisoners left the camp. It was a most unhappy and unfortunate situation but nothing could be done to change the circumstances. Potentially they would be called upon to defend their countries when the situation was under control.

In the meantime, in anticipation, they were placed on training programmes at the Royal Thai Army camp firing ranges at Warin Chamrap. They were issued with 536 rifles with bayonets, seventy-two light machine guns and twenty-seven pistols with 486 rounds of ammunition, together with 125,000 rounds for the machine guns and rifles. This large quantity of firearms was acquired from weapons surrendered by the Japanese.

To keep their spirits up throughout this uncertain time, they relied on several entertainers who took over the theatre. On 13 October, a 'Dutch National' show was performed for their Thai hosts and officials from the Ubon authorities. The show included West Indian calypsos, Javanese dancing, western-European dancing and a clog dance. Without having the precise resources for the production, the performers had to improvise but all agreed it was a great success. They also continued to enjoy the weekly horse-racing meetings in Thung Si Muang and socialising in the centre of Ubon.

Soldaat Henk Gideonse writes that his friend met a local English-speaking girl and describes how he dined with her and bought her presents. When the opportunity arose to make the relationship more intimate, he found out she was not the sort of girl he would have been proud to introduce to his mother!

The Dutch were free to do as they pleased in the town and often visited the cinema, where they viewed newsreels flown in from Bangkok showing events from around the world. On one occasion they saw a newsreel reporting British troops arriving home from the Far East and being reunited with their families. It led them to think about where their families might be, or even if they were still alive. They were on the winning side, of course, but they began to doubt if they were victorious. They had freedom, decent clothing, shoes and food but they were still in a prison camp, sleeping on bamboo beds in huts they had made when they were Prisoners of War.

During their period of imprisonment some Prisoners, probably those based at the aerodrome, had come into contact with a diminutive young lady who owned a small shop selling fruit and roasted cashew nuts. Her name was Khun Yai Lhai Sirichat and her shop was close to where the Prisoners ferried Japanese supplies back and forth across Ubon's river Mun.

Yai Lhai felt pity for the Prisoners as she witnessed the hardships they had to suffer from the Japanese. With help from her daughter, she left fruit by the banks of the river for the men to take, even though helping them was forbidden by the Japanese, who frequently toured the streets warning residents that they faced severe punishment if they spoke to any of their Prisoners. However, this did not dissuade Yai Lhai and her daughter. They regularly left baskets of bananas, mangos and papaya and other fruit that contained vital vitamins badly needed by the men. Initially, the Japanese guards chased Yai Lhai and her daughter away but, undeterred, they kept returning until an officer relented. Despite the earlier warnings, he told the guards to turn a blind eye and avoid confrontation with the locals.

Some days Yai Lhai filled a basket with surplus fruit and carried it to the river for the men to share; on other days she left a basket or two in a conspicuous place for them to pick up when they returned to camp. British Prisoner Tom Brown worked regularly on transportation at the river and vividly remembers Yai Lhai and her fruit and vegetables shop. He recalls that, with permission from the Japanese guards, she gave him and his mates all the fruit that was just past its best. Tom remembers *'lapping up the pomelos. It was a great help to us'*. He took as much fruit as he could carry back to the camp. Obviously there was not enough to share amongst 3,000 Prisoners, but those lucky enough to be in Tom's circle of friends certainly benefitted.

During their period of enforced stay in Ubon, the Dutch held a reception party to honour Yai Lhai and her daughter to thank them for their generosity and kindness. The reception was held in the 'Relaxation and Development' barracks at the aerodrome in the presence of the all remaining men, the governor of Ubon and other dignitaries. They gave her simple gifts, including a carving in the shape of a food stall, and drawings representing memories of their time in Ubon. Thereafter she became affectionately known as the 'Little Mother of Ubon' and took her place in Ubon's folklore.

In his book *Het Vergeten Leger In De Jungle*, Henk Gideonse suggested that Yai Lhai's generosity and bravery emanated from her Buddhist beliefs, which guided her to always help people in need. She did not ask for thanks, but Henk and his friends were

174

so grateful to her. He was moved by the way that she stood up to, and defended herself against, the oppressive guards. He believed that her bravery amounted to a small victory against the Japanese. It was also an act of compassion towards the Prisoners.

In the 1950s a bridge was built adjacent to the river Mun ferry. Today there is a modern market building called Thetsaban located near the bridge on the northern bank of the river. This market is built on the site of the former home of Ubon's governor. Next to the market is Wat Luang, a working temple which the Prisoners would see easily from the riverbank. About 120 yards further to the east of the temple gates is a short terrace of shops and houses. This is where Yai Lhai and her daughter lived after the bridge was built and the riverside was developed. Her original house was on the riverbank a short distance away, but it had to be demolished to make way for the construction of the flood prevention scheme and riverside development.

Behind the temple and slightly to the east is a block of shops and restaurants on the corner of Thanon Phrommathep and Thanon Luang. This is the site of the original market where Yai Lhai traded, and one of the markets where Prisoners purchased food.

Following the reception for Yai Lhai and her daughter, some of the remaining Dutchmen built a memorial, which was dedicated to the people of Ubon. It is believed that it was located in the south-west corner of Thung Si Muang in the centre of old Ubon opposite the library. A photograph taken in December 1945 (see photo gallery) shows that it was a four-sided brick construction, standing about eight feet tall, sitting on a base about four feet square. An inscription of *EX POW*, referring to the Ex-Prisoners of War, was displayed on its front face and there was possibly an inscribed plaque attached to its base.

Another photograph (see photo gallery), thought to have been taken in the 1960s, shows some obvious differences from the original. The base of the memorial appears to have changed from its original decorative display of plants into a plain concrete bed. The pointing between the bricks appears neglected, though the style of brick seems to be the same. An obvious difference is the style of the lettering, and the letter 'W' is missing. Khun Suwit Koonphul recalls that the original lettering was replaced by bronze letters. The missing 'W' is believed to have been stolen for its scrap value. There is also the addition of a pyramid-shaped cap to the top of the structure, and the height of the monument appears to be slightly smaller. It is believed that on the left side of this monument there was an inscription: *Monument of Merit during the Pacific War (World War Two)*.

Thung Si Muang was at some point redeveloped as a recreational centre, and the memorial was relocated to its present position in the north-eastern corner of the park (see photo gallery). It is obviously a new construction of similar design but much smaller than the original. The bricks are larger, the base is neat, and the pyramid-style cap has been retained. The lettering is absent.

There are two structures either side of the pillar. Each one has a metal plate with a brief narrative of the Monument of Merit story, one written in English and the other in Thai. The narrative is copied below exactly as it appears on the plaque, including the unfortunate errors of fact.

The Monument of Merit
In 1941 Japanese troop occupied Thailand and took many allied Prisoners of War Ubon Ratchathani province was one of many areas in Thailand where allied Prisoners of War were kept and forced into hard labour. The Prisoners consisted mainly Australian, British, New Zealand and French nationals, who were tormented towards the allied Prisoners of War physically and mentally by their captors. Being actively sympathetic food, clothes and others, people risk their lives to help them by providing support. As a result, many Thais received harsh punishment form the Japanese soldiers. When the war was over in 1943 many Prisoners of War were freed. Survival due to the assistance of the local people. To show their gratitude, the former Prisoners built this monument to the kindness, generosity and goodwill displayed by the people of Ubon Ratchathani. That is why this monument is called "The Monument of Merit".

176

Although the monument was built by the Dutch and many – if not all – of the British, Australian and American men were unaware of it, the sentiment of the inscription expresses genuine gratitude from all the men to the people of Ubon. Today it serves as a reminder to Ubon that acts of altruism are an important part in daily life for those with Buddhist beliefs. These sentiments are commemorated each year at the 11 November Service of Remembrance.

In October 1945, those remaining Dutchmen who were considered fit and competent enough to fight were selected to return to the Dutch East Indies and transferred to one of six designated camps at Chonburi, Saraburi, Tha Muang, Bangkok, Petchaburi and Nakon Phathom. Training continued, but the men became increasingly frustrated as the dates to return to Java were postponed several times. Eventually, in February 1946, they were dispatched not for Java, but Bali and Lombok. The number of Dutch ex-Prisoners remaining in Thailand on 25 October 1945 was 11,096.

Incidents in French Indochina

When Major Smiley returned to the Candle area following his recovery from his accident, he assigned Major Peter Kemp to Nakhon Phanom on the river Mekong. Opposite Nakhon Phanom in French Indochina was the village of Thakhek, where there was a small Japanese garrison. Also in the village was a group of French civilian internees being held against their will and in possible danger. Major Kemp's priority was to secure their release and safety.

In the group were eighteen women, five men (including a priest), fourteen children and five nuns looking after forty Eurasian orphans. The Japanese originally captured them and turned them over to the Laotian authorities at the end of the hostilities. The situation was further complicated when two nationalist groups entered Thakhek. They were the Free Lao, who were supporters of the Lao royal family, and the Annamites from Vietnam who were loyal to Ho Chi Minh. Both were opposed to the French returning to power and wanted to keep the internees as hostages.

The Laotians, who were loyal to the French, were poorly equipped and unable to protect the internee group. They handed them over to the French, but they also struggled against the nationalists. The Annamites gained control of the group, who were becoming increasingly frightened. It was a delicate situation requiring skill, diplomacy and decisive action to bring the internees to safety.

On arrival at Nakhon Phanom, Major Kemp wrote to Captain Nakajima the Japanese commander in Thakhek with an appeal to make men available to protect the group. He also sent a letter to the Annamite leader appealing for calm and asking that the internees were not harmed. He then travelled to Ubon to discuss the situation with Major Smiley. They both returned to Nakhon Phanom and crossed the river with Khun Thawin Soonthornsaradul, the town's governor, and Lieutenant Klotz from the French Special Services. When they arrived, the governor of Thakhek took them to the convent where the internees were being held. Their leader, Madame Collin, told them that her husband had been beheaded and the Annamite rebels were increasingly threatening, making them fear for their lives.

Major Smiley and Lieutenant Klotz were taken to meet the Annamite leader, whilst Major Kemp stayed with the hostages. Two hours later, after an acrimonious exchange of views, Major Smiley returned and confirmed that the civilians would be taken back to the safety of Nakhon Phanom.

As they were preparing to leave, a Japanese patrol arrived and arrested the three officers. They were marched to Captain Nakajima's office; he claimed he had not received the terms of the surrender treaty and he could not release the internees without specific orders from his superiors. Despite protests, he bluntly refused to release them.

Major Smiley decided to return to Ubon to obtain the required orders. Before he left, he insisted that Japanese guards replace the Annamites and that Captain Nakajima should accept full responsibility for the safety of the internees. Captain Nakajima agreed and they returned to the convent to order the change of guard.

Whilst this was taking place one of the Japanese guards, who was obviously drunk, attempted to wrench a wristwatch from one of the nuns. As Major Smiley intervened, the guard drew out his bayonet whereupon Major Kemp felt for his pistol. Luckily the guard's corporal was nearby; he grabbed the soldier's arm and overpowered him. The soldier was slapped about the face by the corporal and he stumbled out of the room. Major Smiley reported the incident to Captain Nakajima, who ordered the soldier into his office and slapped him again before he was marched away. Major Smiley then set off for Ubon, whilst Major Kemp and Lieutenant Klotz stayed with the internees.

At the convent, Major Kemp and Lieutenant Klotz received news that another group of French civilians were being held against their will at the mining village of Phon Tiou, about twenty-five miles north of Thakhek. Lieutenant Klotz commandeered an old Citroën car and together they drove through the hills and forests to the village. They were greeted by a desperate French lady who led them to her house. Inside they found her teenage daughter and a terrified neighbour, both of whom had received gunshot wounds.

The lady explained that on 22 August Japanese soldiers, who may have been deserters, had broken into their houses, stolen possessions and then opened fire, seriously injuring her daughter and neighbour and fatally wounding the neighbour's wife. She also said that there were more French internees at the Bartholony mines in the town of Boneng, a few miles away. Major Kemp and Lieutenant Klotz had to prioritise the injured at Phon Tiou and return to the situation of the Boneng internees at a later date.

The old Citroën was too small to carry everyone comfortably, especially the casualties, and the condition of the road was very poor. It was late in the day and darkness was falling, so they had to leave quickly. When the car's battery started to fail, the headlights were too dim to see the road ahead and they were forced to find somewhere to stay for the night. Luckily they saw a small hut and, after carefully approaching it, met a friendly and hospitable Lao who, after listening to their plight, invited them to stay for the night. He had very little to offer them but they were relieved to be safe. Fortunately the car was working again by the afternoon of the following day, and they slowly made their way to Thakhek.

By the time they arrived at Thakhek, Major Smiley had returned from Ubon with orders for Captain Nikajima to release the internees. Major Rowland had also arrived from his posting at Nong Khai to reinforce the situation. The internees, the injured casualties and the officers returned to Nakhon Phanom without incident. The ex-internees stayed at the hospital until their repatriation instructions were received. Although the two casualties from Phon Tiou were made comfortable, the doctors did not have the instruments or the anaesthetic with which to operate. After they were transferred to Ubon, the injured were eventually air-lifted to Bangkok and, after successful surgery, made full recoveries.

Meanwhile, on the 11 September, Major Kemp, Major Smiley and Lieutenant Klotz returned to Thakhek and then travelled onwards to Boneng to rescue the beleaguered French civilians. This time Captain Nakajima co-operated by providing a reliable lorry and an escort.

As they approached the mine, they heard gunfire coming from the school building in which a small unit of Franco-Laotian soldiers were defending the civilians against about 150 Annamite rebels. The three officers, flanked by their Japanese escort, walked boldly towards the school and confidently, if somewhat optimistically, ordered a ceasefire. The surprised Annamite commander was uncertain but, after a long pause, ordered his men to stand down.

Major Smiley then walked up to the school and spoke with the French officer inside. His small section of twelve personnel was defending seven very frightened civilians: one male, four females and two children. After negotiations with the rebels, the civilians were released and they returned to Nakhon Phanom without further incident.

Major Smiley sent the following message to HQs at Kandy and Rangoon:

Now that the lives of about one hundred women and children have been saved from certain death at Annamite or Jap [sic] hands I wish to make the following comments. I strongly recommend the untiring and courageous work of Kemp and Klotz of E group. I again express my gratitude to the governor and officials of Nakon Phnom [sic] for their work and kindness shown to all. The Annamites in FIC I consider an element hostile to not only the French but the British as well.

All known French civilians in the area were now safe and waiting for repatriation, but that was not the end of trouble in Thakhek.

Shortly after the French civilians arrived in Nakhon Phanom, a message arrived from HQ stating that SEAC would take control in French Indochina south of the sixteenth parallel, and the Chinese would take control of the area to the north. As Thakhek was to the north, Major Kemp was expecting Chinese troops to arrive at any time. There was growing acrimony between the French and the Chinese. which made Major Kemp's position difficult because he (and the British) were allied with both sides. Despite this, he was still advised to approach the Chinese with reasonable caution.

Added to this, the Americans were opposed to France retaking French Indochina in the post-war settlement. Although the Americans did not have any authority from SEAC to be present in north-east Thailand, a small OSS unit of ten officers and NCOs, under the command of Major Bank, arrived at Nong Khai. They crossed the river to Vientiane and demanded the French stop their aggression towards both the Annamese and Free Laos Movement. They then moved to Nakhon Phanom, where they cruelly lied to the French internees at the hospital that they were about to return to Thakhek. Instead of behaving like a friends and ally, the American Major was working directly against the French and Major Kemp without any authority.

The OSS group crossed the river to Thakhek, where they found the Japanese had departed and the Annamites had made the French ineffective. Despite Major Kemp's protests, Major Bank encouraged the Annamese to pursue their struggle for freedom from the French. A provocative situation was evolving.

On 27 September, Major Kemp and Lieutenant Klotz opted to take some much-needed supplies to French troops, which meant passing through Thakhek. Major Bank had already told Lieutenant Klotz to stay away but, according to official directives, there was no reason why he should. They took a launch over the river and helpfully took on board a Lieutenant Reese, who was one of Major Bank's personnel.

When they arrived at Thakhek, the Annamites refused entry to Lieutenant Klotz and warned him that he was to be arrested. There was a heated exchange of words between Major Kemp and the Annamite leader, during which Lieutenant Reese was joined by three more OSS officers from his unit. Instead of helping Major Kemp, they watched as the ugly situation evolved.

Deciding to prevent the situation from worsening, Major Kemp and Lieutenant Klotz turned to walk back to the launch. Major Kemp deliberately walked behind Lieutenant Klotz to protect him from the gunmen but it was not enough: one of the gunmen ran at the two men and thrust his rifle under Major Kemp's armpit. He shot Lieutenant Klotz in the back at point-blank range. Major Kemp stumbled into the launch carrying the Lieutenant, who died in his arms. The Americans did nothing, but they were shocked at what they had witnessed. Their excuse was that they were obeying orders from Major Bank.

Lieutenant Klotz was buried with full military honours in Nakhon Phanom's Catholic cemetery. Lieutenant Reece apparently had some sort of a conscience because, against the advice of Major Kemp, he attended the funeral. He stood alone in the graveyard and faced the hatred directed at him. After the service he saluted and marched away. The grave was marked with a simple cross, but it had to be continually replaced after Annamese sympathisers living in the town uprooted it in cowardly acts of disrespect.

Major Smiley arrived in Nakhon Phanom shortly after the funeral and was debriefed by Major Kemp. A message was sent to Major Bank requesting an urgent meeting the next day. Major Smiley went to Thakhek alone and was greeted by a gushing Major Bank who expressed condolences for Lieutenant Klotz. Major Smiley took an immediate dislike to him and, after an inconclusive meeting, returned across the river. He sent a priority message to Calcutta HQ requesting Major Banks and his unit be removed from the area immediately. Simultaneously, the French government formally protested to Washington DC in the strongest terms about the pro-nationalist support from American officers in Laos.

In a letter dated 2 October, General Leclerc wrote to Major Mackenzie at Force 136 HQ: (Translated)

I learn of the loyal and courageous conduct of Major Kemp, who, in Thakhek, seeing Lieutenant Klotz threatened by armed Annamites, did not hesitate to put himself between this officer and the aggressors in an attempt to save his life. Unable to succeed, he was able to bring back Lieutenant Klotz's body. I want to tell you how much we appreciated this noble attitude of Major Kemp's fighting camaraderie. Would you like to convey to him all our gratitude and my warmest congratulations?
Please accept, Sir, the assurance of my most cordial feelings.
Leclerc

In his autobiography, Major Smiley later reflected that post-war American policy espoused anti-colonialism to such an extent that they were either prepared to support all anti-colonial groups, or they were so naïve they did not realise they were helping Communist movements such as the Annamites. The French eventually gave up Indochina and the Dutch left the East Indies; this, he concluded, may have been a consequence of the policy that contributed to the war in Vietnam a few years later.

At the beginning of October, Major Bank was ordered to withdraw from Laos. His behaviour was described by Major Smiley as despicable. Major Bank later became the founder of the US Army Special Forces, also known as the Green Berets.

In mid-October, the French ex-internees were transferred to Ubon where they recuperated and enjoyed Ubon's finest hospitality, including the Dutch theatre performances. They later travelled by train to Bangkok.

The Japanese

Ubon was designated as one of eight concentration centres throughout Thailand where Japanese soldiers were ordered to surrender and hand in their weapons. The other centres were located at Bangkok, Lampang, Chiang Mai, Nakhon Pathon, Ban Pong, Kanchanaburi and Nakhon Nayok.

The Royal Thai Army and the Allied 7th Indian Division 114 Indian Brigade under the command of Major Smiley, were responsible for guarding the Japanese in Ubon until their repatriation was arranged.

The Japanese military units stationed in Ubon were reported to consist of the 4th Air Sector HQ (81), 75th Air Battalion (358), 112th Airfield Construction Unit and the 84th Airfield Battalion. Unfortunately, numbers in each unit are not quoted but the overall numbers of Japanese personnel began to increase as they arrived in Ubon to surrender. It was reported that there were

9,200 Japanese remaining in north-east Thailand, mainly under the command of Lieutenant-General Hirata.

Following their surrender in August it was generally anticipated, with some justification, that the Japanese would mount a hostile reaction towards the Allies, and the Prisoners in particular. Fortunately, they accepted their fate and resigned themselves to defeat. Whilst they were in Ubon, both Colonel Toosey and Major Smiley commented that there was little trouble from the Japanese and discipline was generally good, with officers obeying orders without question. Any occasional isolated incident was usually the result of drinking too much alcohol. On one such occasion in a drunken brawl at an Ubon brothel, a Japanese private attacked an officer and left him with a vicious bite.

It is perhaps not surprising that some Japanese and Korean soldiers decided to desert. Five Japanese deserted the Ubon camp on 21 October and Major Kemp recalls there were Japanese deserters in the countryside around Thakhek. What became of them is not known; that they mingled into the Thai community is unlikely, given the level of hatred the Thais had for Japanese military. It is possible they found their way home, which they would have done anyway if they had remained in camp. Some may have offered their services to the nationalist armies of French Indochina. Most had been away from their homes for many years and were weary of fighting. They just wanted to return home quickly without creating further problems for themselves.

At Savvanakhet in French Indochina, opposite Mukdahan on the river Mekong, a Japanese garrison became aware that the Chinese were to take control of the area north of the sixteenth parallel and decided to go to Ubon where they surrendered.

The Japanese gave up their weapons to the Royal Thai Army and 7/2 Punjab Regiment under the command of Major K. McCutcheon. Some Japanese soldiers were selected for essential guard duties at the camp and specific fuel dumps and were trusted to retain their weapons.

Major Peter Kemp recalls in his memoir that 400 rifles and 20,000 rounds of ammunition were divided between Nakhon Phanom and Mukdahan. They were then dispatched to remaining pockets of the French military who were attempting to restore order in French Indochina at Thakhek and Savannakhet. Another consignment of 200 rifles and ammunition was sent to French forces in Pakse, to help maintain order. Other quantities were used for training purposes by the Royal Thai Army and the Dutch.

In his final report Major Smiley noted that there were incidents where Japanese Prisoners had purposely disposed of their rifles by throwing them into the river or burying underground.

By early November, all Japanese guns and ammunition had been collected by the Royal Thai Army. Inventories were efficiently written in triplicate and easily checked against the neatly laid out rows of armoury. Once counted, the guns and ammunition were transferred to secure storage at Warin barracks. After consulting Major-General Evans in Bangkok, a plan was authorised to take all arms by rail to Bangkok docks where they were loaded on LCTs (Landing Craft Tanks), taken out to sea in the Gulf of Thailand and thrown overboard.

The Japanese also handed over one hundred tons of aerial bombs, mines and grenades. The decision to dispose of this ammunition took longer to confirm. Anecdotally, it was the Royal Air Force who had the responsibility of deciding if the bombs were useful or not. Although reaching a decision took some time, it was finally agreed to destroy everything at Ubon. This task was given Major Hedley, who had arrived at Ubon to assist Major Smiley in early September. He decided that the airstrip built by the Prisoners at Ban Nong Phai was the perfect site to discharge the bombs. He had previously inspected the airstrip and found several trenches had been excavated across its width. The chilling fact was that the Prisoners had previously dug out these trenches thinking they were doing so to prevent Allied aircraft from landing but it was later revealed that they would have been executed and buried in the trenches if the Allies had invaded Thailand.

Major Hedley ordered a ton of munitions to be placed in each of three of the trenches. Fuses were set to ignite three explosions separately over a thirty-second period. After the bombs were ceremoniously blown up, three large craters remained. A further two tons were placed in each crater, and so on, until everything was discharged. Advanced warnings were circulated and it was reported that the blasts could be felt six miles away in Ubon. The entire cache of one hundred tons was disposed of apparently without any accidents. However, Khun Thongdee Wongman remembers his friend was killed whilst playing with a grenade at the airstrip. A small selection of fragments and a bomb casing was recovered in 2019.

It was agreed that the Japanese would be trusted to guard all stores, especially fuel dumps, but theft was an ongoing problem and it was chiefly local Thais who were looking for opportunities to prosper. Major Smiley constantly asked the Japanese guards why they did not open fire to deter suspected thieves. The Japanese replied that they would do so next time, but they did not. Despite reassurances, perhaps the Japanese thought that if they killed someone who was stealing they would be arrested and found guilty of murder. Then, on the night of 19 and 20 October 1945, a Japanese guard shot dead a local Thai attempting to steal from a fuel dump.

The following morning, a party of officials from the police, army and government followed Major Smiley to the scene. They held a roadside enquiry, where it was established that two Japanese guards had come into contact with two suspected looters and approached them to find out what they were doing. The suspects could not speak Japanese and the guards could not speak Thai, but apparently the guards' approach was polite and civil. However, one of the looters took the offensive and attacked a guard with a large stick, hitting him violently about the head.

After the resulting heated exchange of words, a shot was fired which hit one of the Thais. His accomplice disappeared into the darkness but the injured one staggered along the road until he fell and died.

Major Smiley's group followed the trail of blood along the road and, after confirming the looter was dead, acquitted the guards and commended them for their action. After this incident, the Japanese realised that the British and Thai authorities supported them in doing their job and they would not be held guilty of murder.

The governor agreed that the deterrent of being shot dead was far greater than the prospect of making a small profit from looting. Although further attempts to steal from the camps and fuel dumps were reduced following this incident, they were not eliminated entirely. The railway station was a prime target, especially after a delivery of supplies from Bangkok was unloaded and stored. One Thai was caught at the station stealing copper; he pleaded guilty and was sentenced to eighteen months' imprisonment in Ubon jail.

Before they surrendered, the Japanese intended to build an air-training centre and workshops at Pakse in French Indochina. They transported machinery by rail from Bangkok to Ubon and continued the journey by road. As the war ended, consignments of machinery were abandoned by the side of the road. Major Hedley considered that the assortment of lathes, compressors and other machinery would be useful in Great Britain where there was a scarcity. Some of the Japanese in the Ubon camp, supervised by British army engineers, were sent out to recover the machines. Even though motor transport was limited and in poor condition because of lack of spare parts, they used imagination and ingenuity to move the machinery back to Ubon, some of which weighed up to three tons. Everything was sent to Bangkok by rail but whether it finally reached Great Britain and was put to good use is unknown.

Gradually the Japanese were transferred to the Nakhon Nayok concentration area, seventy miles north east of the centre of Bangkok. One report stated that on 18 November 1,100 Japanese left Ubon, but there were obviously more transfers at other times. The numbers sent over were probably limited by the passenger capacity any particular train could carry safely. There is no record of whether they travelled in ordinary train carriages or in wagons.

It was good news that Ubon was being liberated at last from the strain on its economy and resources because of the enforced obligation to house the Japanese. Towards the end of 1945, a small contingent of Japanese remained to look after and guard equipment before transferring it to Nakhon Nayok. Most Japanese had returned to Japan by August 1946.

During the fighting Japanese military vehicles were in high demand in the west of Thailand where the need was far greater because of the concentrated military presence. With a corresponding shortage of vehicles in Ubon, the Japanese used horses to travel around the region. Moreover, horses could often move more easily through densely vegetated countryside than motor transport. When Major Smiley arrived in Ubon, the Japanese had in their possession 1,252 horses. Some had been driven overland and arrived with the Japanese and some had been purchased locally in Ubon. (A 1934–1935 census estimation of the number of horses in the Ubon area was 25,620. There were also 363,608 head of cattle, 300,903 buffaloes and twelve elephants.)

After inspecting the horses, Major Smiley angrily accused the Japanese of keeping them in the same diabolical conditions, and treating them with the same disrespect and contempt, as they had their human Prisoners. The poor animals were starved, sick and injured and many were on the point of death. They had not been given sufficient feed and were forced to eat their own droppings. Saddle sores were infected, many had fetid ulcers and they were dying at a rate of ten per day. It was a horrible and distressing sight, and a situation that demanded immediate humane action.

With the help of ex-Prisoner Tom Phillips, who was a racehorse trainer before the war, they extracted 628 wretched animals to be immediately and mercifully put down by a single bullet to the head.

Being in the Royal Horse Guards and owner of thoroughbred horses, Major Smiley had a great affection for horses; the state of these poor animals, together with his decision to shoot them personally, caused him great distress. A group of Thais from the village asked him to stop the slaughter because, as Buddhists, it was against their belief to kill animals. In his most diplomatic manner, and with great sadness, he explained that he regretted his actions but he was bringing an end to the horses' suffering out of a sense of duty and his utmost respect for them.

In an unexpected outburst, the Japanese accused him of taking revenge on the horses because the Allies had won the war. Major Smiley vented his anger at this accusation by calling them to parade. With the help of an interpreter, Sergeant Thomas, he told them in no uncertain terms that the horses had to be shot because it was the Japanese ill-treatment and lack of care that put them in such a hopeless condition in the first place.

Reports that Major Smiley was shooting a large number of horses quickly reached HQ in Bangkok. His superiors were alarmed and responded by sending Lieutenant Colonel Gulsher Khan of the 7th Indian Division to check the remaining horses. After he saw their condition, he agreed that an additional 483 should be shot forthwith. Only 130 survived.

Unfortunately, the incident did not end there. Tom Phillips had left the camp so Major Smiley ordered some Japanese so-called veterinary surgeons to help him shoot the horses but they were hopeless. Instead of taking one shot to the head, they were taking two or three; even so, it appeared that some horses were being buried alive. Major Smiley stopped them and continued to shoot the horses himself with his American .30 carbine. He was physically sick after he finished this most unpleasant task.

Routine Duties

In September, Major John Hedley was assigned to work with Major Smiley and the Royal Thai Army in supervising the Japanese surrender and disarmament. He had already spent two years as Intelligence Officer with the 111 Chindit Brigade in Burma where he was posted behind enemy lines for two months until he was injured. After his recovery, he was transferred to Force 136 and entered Burma again behind enemy lines. He met up with the British advance and was awarded the Distinguished Service Order for his actions. After the war ended, he left Force 136 and joined 207 British Military Mission to assist in repatriating British ex-POWs.

When he arrived in Ubon, he had the appearance of an eccentric character: he walked at a very fast pace with an old .303 Lee Enfield rifle slung over his shoulder and wearing a distinctive Australian Terai hat. He was nicknamed the 'Mad Major', not least because he displayed no tact or patience with the Thais. This often led to complaints; Major Smiley had to smooth over these and apologise to the offended complainants on Major Hedley's behalf. But the two officers worked well together, and Major Hedley was a great help during Major Smiley's absence from Ubon. Although he could speak some Thai, he received further tutoring from government schoolmaster Professor Nielson, who was from Denmark but resident in Ubon throughout the war. He was the only person in town who could fluently speak English and Thai, and so was a great help with interpretation.

Major Hedley stayed at the Royal Thai Army base at Warin Chamrap. Each day was different for him but usually he took the ferry across the river Mun to attend a briefing meeting at the police station, where the day's business was discussed and the previous day's activities reported. The journey often took forty-five minutes because the river was running high and wide following the monsoon. Major Smiley chaired these meetings if he was in Ubon. The other participants included officers from the

191

Royal Thai Army, the Japanese army, local government and the police.

Major Hedley took responsibility for the Japanese Army and was tasked with disarming them and concentrating them into a secure, well-guarded area. In his memoir he recalls that the majority of the Japanese in his charge were fighting the Chinese in Shanghai at the end of 1943. In mid-1944 they moved to Canton (now called Guangzhou, near Hong Kong) and from there marched to Ubon, a distance of almost 800 miles. It took them more than a year to do so and they continued fighting the Chinese as they progressed. Their commanding officer was Lieutenant-General Hirata and the Divisional Chief of Staff was Colonel Hotta.

Providing adequate accommodation for more than 9,000 Japanese troops had to be resolved, especially as it was uncertain how long they would be held. They needed water and they also had to be secure to prevent desertion and protect the people of Ubon. The perfect location was found just north of the aerodrome on the proposed site of Ubon university, but the Thai authorities objected as they had already started building construction. (This is now the site of Ubon Rajabhat university; one of the original buildings occupied by the Japanese still remains.) The authorities were over-ruled but construction of the camp was delayed because there was a shortage of suitable materials. The governor acquired some supplies through his contacts, and a useful source was provided by recycling materials used by the Japanese in building accommodation elsewhere in Ubon, possibly including the Prisoners' former camp.

Major Hedley was at the centre of most activities and he said that his work was interesting and varied, although he was possibly frustrated by the Thai authorities who discovered that his pace of working was far quicker than anything they had dealt with before. He had to accept that there was a difference in culture.

Major Smiley's remit was to deal with all situations regardless of whether they were distressing, pleasant, stressful or amusing.

To help him he had the reliable support of several other British officers and Thai civilians. He had no misgivings about confiscating items from the Japanese, whether they were personal or military. He took cars (in particular a straight-eight Cadillac and a 1942 Chevrolet Drophead Coupé), binoculars, pistols and swords. He gave some of the items to his staff as reward for their work and service.

One such person was a boatman from Nong Khai. At an evening dinner party, Major Smiley presented him with a Japanese sword as a reward for his gun-running trips across the Mekong. Later that same evening, the boatman returned to the dining room carrying the sword dripping with blood. His story was that he had found a thief in the storeroom and, without any misgiving, cut off his head. In disbelief, Major Smiley went to investigate. It was true.

On some occasions Major Smiley was summoned to Bangkok for meetings at HQ. He usually travelled in an aircraft provided by Wing-Commander Manop Souriya, also known as 'Nobby', from the Royal Thai Air Force. Before the war Nobby had trained at West Point in the United States and spent some time attached to the Royal Air Force. Major Smiley recalls that the aircraft Nobby provided was a Mitsubishi Advanced Trainer.

Theoretically flying should have made travel more convenient but on one particular occasion, on 31 October, Major Smiley was allocated an aircraft which had reportedly spent a lot time under repair, either at Ubon or Korat. He and Major Kemp were to be flown to Bangkok by Pilot Officer Prang, a rather unsettling name for a pilot and perhaps a forewarning of what was in store.

The first leg of the trip, from Nakhon Phanom to Udon Thani, was uneventful; they simply followed the laterite road at a height of 1,000 feet. The second leg was to Korat, about 200 miles to the south. This time they flew at 5,000 feet and navigated by following the Petchabun mountain range and the Korat plateau. Although the views were spectacular, it was not a place for the unreliable Mitsubishi to falter, which, of course, it did. The engine backfired and cut out leaving it to glide towards the mountains. After pilot Prang had furiously twiddled and twisted various switches, knobs and handles, the engine sparked into life and they laboured on.

The engine died five more times, with a loss of height between each stall. Pilot Prang managed to keep the aircraft airborne until they crash landed at Korat. A wheel broke off and the starboard wing hit the ground in a cloud of red dust. Luckily no one was injured. After a lunch with some strong drinks to steady their nerves, Major Smiley and Major Kemp felt lucky that they were able to continue their journey in another aircraft.

That should have been enough excitement for one trip but there was more drama on the return flight two days later. Nobby found another aircraft, which Major Smiley describes as a low-wing monoplane. Major Smiley flew this aircraft himself, with Major Kemp as passenger, following the same route in reverse. Shortly after take-off from Korat, they hit a large bird and Major Smiley struggled to control the aircraft. The bird had hit the port wing and dented a three-foot section, causing the ailerons to jam, which meant the aircraft could not be safely controlled. Luckily, Major Smiley had retained the skills needed in such an emergency situation and managed to land the aircraft safely.

After a short delay they took off in the same aircraft in which they had previously crash landed. The flight to Nakhon Phanom was uneventful, although after they landed they realised the aircraft had almost run out of fuel.

Although he does not give any details, Major Smiley survived two further airplane accidents, one in which he was a passenger in a Japanese bomber which overturned and broke a wing on landing.

Operation Candle Completed

By early November, Major Smiley's time in Ubon was almost over. He made a special tour of the Candle area to bid farewell and thank the many friends he had made, especially within the ranks of the Seri Thai. He recalls visiting each group where the men who had volunteered to fight the Japanese paraded in his honour. After a rousing farewell speech, each group gave him three *khios* (three cheers). There was one last party and feast, during which he was presented with gifts including engraved silver cigarette boxes. Nai Tiang Sirikhandra then took on the responsibility of disarming and disbanding the Seri Thai guerrillas.

Major Smiley officially relinquished responsibility for Operation Candle and Ubon on 8 November 1945, just over five months after his arrival on 30 May. He left for Bangkok where he spent three weeks on leave and wrote his final operational report. During this relaxing break he met Luang Pridi for the first time and caught up with many of his Seri Thai associates at a number of parties and dinners. He finally left Bangkok with several other SOE officers, including Sergeant Collins, on 11 December 1945. On his return to England, he attended a Staff College course on the personal recommendation of Field Marshall Sir Archibald Wavell (Lord Wavell).

Major Hedley remained in Ubon to finalise outstanding issues. Before the peace treaty ending hostilities between Thailand and Great Britain was signed, Major Hedley and Major Smiley sometimes found themselves in difficult political and diplomatic situations. Although they always received the most courteous co-operation from the Thai authorities, they could not help them legally nor attend any functions in an official capacity because Great Britain was technically still at war with Thailand. For example, it was difficult telling Ubon's governor that he could not have transport when there were scores of Japanese vehicles standing idle. But they always managed to find ways around these problems without breaking the letter of the law. So it was a great relief for Major Hedley when the peace treaty between the two countries was signed on 1 January 1946. To celebrate, a party was held in Ubon that started on 18 January and lasted for three days and nights with continuous dinners, horse racing, theatre performances, dancing and sports.

In early February 1946, Major Hedley travelled to Bangkok to demand payment for a debt owed by Force 136 for quantities of salt provided by the Ubon authorities. He returned with the money and paid it over to the governor. On the 14 February, following a series of leaving parties, he left Ubon by train for the last time. Characteristically, he sat in a Jeep that was loaded onto the last carriage of the train. When he arrived at Korat, he stayed for four days to say more goodbyes and then drove the Jeep to Bangkok. He sailed from Bangkok on 22 February and arrived in England on 15 April.

Ongoing Responsibilities

Major Kemp had already attended meetings in Bangkok to discuss the dissolution of Force 136 in Thailand and his potential future postings in South East Asia. He was asked to take over responsibility for the Candle area from Major Smiley, which he immediately agreed to do. Then, in the middle of November, he attended a meeting in Bangkok with the GOC Major-General Geoffrey Evans to receive further orders. Major-General Evans was a highly regarded and experienced officer who had previously commanded a brigade at the battle of Imphal. He was now commander of the 7th Indian Division and all British troops in Thailand in the immediate post-war period.

By now Ubon was slowly getting back normal. Major Smiley had gone, and Major Kemp and Major Hedley's tasks and daily routines were under control. However, the French command in Saigon were still struggling to make contact with many of their forces in Laos and they requested help from the British. Major-General Evans agreed to assist by sending in troops if required; he sent orders to Major Kemp to gather and grade intelligence from the Candle area and to be on standby to help if required. They were the only British forces remaining in the north and east of Korat, but Ubon was not close enough to French Indochina to be of any help. Major Kemp made his base at Nakhon Phanom where he could monitor the situation at Thakhek and be available if necessary at the other border towns of Nong Khai and Mukdahan.

The French, the Annamites and Free Lao guerrillas continued to clash almost daily across the Mekong in French Indochina. There was an ugly situation at Nakhon Phanom where several Franco-Laotian soldiers who had returned to their homes on leave mysteriously disappeared. Some of them were found beheaded and others were also believed to have been murdered. Major Kemp was ambushed several times and fired upon by snipers who were, luckily for him, poor shots and always failed to follow up their attacks. The immediate post-war period was a turbulent and troubled time in this area.

The peace treaty between Thailand and Great Britain provided for the immediate withdrawal of all missions supported by British forces, and this included Major Kemp. Fortunately, the French had recovered their positions in French Indochina and were adequately supported from Saigon so the need for Major Kemp's support along the Mekong border towns was no longer required. On 20 January 1946 he and his unit left Nakhon Phanom in convoy on their final journey to Ubon, calling at Mukdahan along the way. At Ubon they transferred their transport and stores to the Royal Thai Army, under the supervision of Major Hedley. Although the records do not confirm the specific location of where Major Kemp was staying, it is assumed it was close to Major Hedley at the Royal Thai Army barracks at Warin Chamrap. They had a few days rest and recuperation before they departed for Bangkok by train on the 23 January.

Major Kemp made good use of his three days leave in Ubon. On the second night he was in the company of Major Hedley, an Australian from the War Graves Commission, and some British sappers who were passing through Ubon on a road-reconnaissance exercise. They played poker; during the course of the evening Major Hedley, although he was a teetotaller, made sure there was a copious supply of *lao kao*, the potent Thai whisky. The party ended around midnight and Major Kemp decided to clear his head by taking a walk.

Sometime later, he woke up with a splitting headache in a hut that he did not recognise. As he regained his senses, he realised his trousers, underwear, socks and shoes were missing but strangely he was still wearing his shirt. His wallet remained in his shirt pocket, together with his identification papers. There was nothing in the room apart from a piece of rancid sacking upon which he was lying.

His immediate thoughts returned to a previous incident two years earlier in Albania that had left him feeling dizzy and confused in the same way he was now feeling. He deduced he had been attacked and hit on the head. As he was gathering his thoughts an elderly Thai man, presumably the owner of the hut, entered the room, looked at him, smirked and left.

If he had been attacked, as he feared, it was probably because there was still a bounty on his head from the Annamite rebels in Thakhek. He decided to make his escape whilst he could and wrapped the rancid sacking round his waist like a sarong to protect his modesty. Not knowing in which direction to run, he blindly followed his instinct. He was lucky and arrived at the barracks and found his way to his billet.

The next day an intelligence report emerged stating that Viet Minh agents living in Ubon were keeping Major Kemp and his unit under surveillance. He surmised that it was they who had attacked him whilst he was taking some fresh air and, after knocking him unconscious, had taken him to the room belonging to the elderly Thai. The bounty was worth more if he was handed over alive rather than dead. Presumably the agents were badly prepared for the encounter and had no means with which to tie him up so, they had left him in the safe house without his clothes in the hope he would remain unconscious or, when he regained consciousness, be too embarrassed to escape. It is assumed that these agents then disappeared to find a Viet Minh commander with whom they would return to the house.

It was a strange event and the real story will never be discovered; even the speculation about what happened is uncertain but fortunately Major Kemp survived and was able to continue by train with his unit to Bangkok.

Whilst in Bangkok he was offered the command of a mission to Lombok and Bali in the Dutch East Indies, which he immediately accepted. SEAC were planning to send a small advance party to report on the situation on the islands because the Japanese had not surrendered and the local population were rising up against the reinstatement of Dutch rule. After enjoying the delights of Bangkok, he left for his new, exacting posting on 15 February 1946.

After the last group of Japanese soldiers had caught the train to Bangkok, Ubon returned to normal. Transport and communications slowly improved and the region returned to its agricultural way of life. Then, in 1961, the Americans arrived at the Royal Thai Air Force base at Ubon for covert operations in the Vietnam war. The Australians arrived two years later.

Another chapter in Ubon's history had begun.

Chapter 18

CONSEQUENCES AND TRAGEDY

The War Crimes Trial of Major Chida Sotomatsu

Before Major Chida Sotomatsu arrived as camp commander at Ubon he commanded several other camps in Thailand. Between August 1942 and October 1942 he commanded the Number 1 Group of Prisoners, between October 1942 and March 1943 the Number 4 Group, and he returned to command Number 1 Group from March 1943 until August 1945.

He was singled out to stand trial at Singapore Military Court accused of war crimes. His trial began on 21 October and ended on 3 December 1946. He was charged, with others, with the following taken from War Crimes Trials records:

Charge 1: Committing a war crime in that they between 1 October 1942 and 1 August 1944 while engaged in the administration of British, Australian and Dutch Prisoners of War employed in the construction and maintenance of the Thailand-Burma railway were, in violation of the laws and usages of war, concerned in the inhumane treatment of the said Prisoners of War resulting in the deaths of many of the said Prisoners of War and physical suffering by many others of the said Prisoners of War.

Charge 2: Committing a war crime in that they between 1 October 1942 and 1 August 1944 were, in violation of the laws and usages of war, concerned in the employment of the labour of British, Australian and Dutch Prisoners of War in work having connection with the operation of the War that is to say the construction and maintenance of a railway from Nong Pladuk to Thanbyuzayat (commonly known as the Thailand-Burma railway) for the purpose of transporting supplies and munitions to the Japanese forces fighting in Burma.

Charge 3: Committing a war crime in that they between 1 October 1942 and 1 August 1944 while engaged in the administration of British, Australian and Dutch Prisoners of War employed in the construction and maintenance of the Burma–Thailand railway were, in violation of the laws and usages of war, concerned in the employment of the labour of the said Prisoners of War in work which was excessive having regard to the rank and capacity of the said Prisoners of War.

Charge 4: Committing a war crime in that they between 1 October 1942 and 1 August 1944 while engaged in the administration of British, Australian and Dutch Prisoners of War employed in the construction and maintenance of the Thailand-Burma railway were, in violation of the laws and usages of war, concerned in the internment of the said Prisoners of War in conditions which were unhealthy and unhygienic.

Charge 8: (to Major Chida Sotomatsu only): Committing a war crime in that he in Thailand between the first day of August 1944 and the fourth day of December 1944, when in command of a group of Prisoners of War, was, in violation of the laws and usages of war, concerned in the employment of British, Australian and Dutch Prisoners of War at Nong Pladuk No. 1 camp in work having connection with the operation of the War that is to say:
The maintenance and working of the Thailand-Burma railway for the purpose of transporting munitions and supplies to the Japanese Fighting Forces,
The handling and loading of the munitions and supplies aforesaid. Thereby exposing them to aerial bombardment resulting in the deaths of approximately 104 Prisoners of War and physical injury to many others.

The specific date relating to charge eight is 6 September 1944. On this date the Allies bombed the railway sidings at Camp 1 Nong Pladuk. Ninety-eight British and Dutch POWs were killed and more than 200 wounded, some severely. In the weeks prior to the air raid, the Prisoners had made numerous requests to construct shelters and slit trenches for their protection during an air raid. Major Chida refused permission.

Camp 1 was adjacent to the railway. During the raid the Prisoners were ordered to move trucks containing ammunition to a safer distance but at great risk to themselves. Some weeks later, Major Chida relented and gave his permission to build shelters and dig slit trenches. In November there was another raid, but fortunately this time there was no casualties. However, in a further raid on 3 December, six Prisoners were killed and fifteen wounded, some of whom died later.

Major Chida was found guilty of charges one to four. He was also found guilty of charge number eight, but it was amended to delete the words 'resulting in the deaths of approximately 104 Prisoners of War and physical injury to many others'. On 3 December 1946 he was sentenced to ten years imprisonment.

Between 5 and 7 February 1946, Major Chida stood trial again on three further charges relating to cruelly beating and maltreating eight British officers. In the third charge it was stated that two officers had died as a result. These crimes were committed in September 1943 at Kanburi camp. Major Chida stated in his defence that he took no part in the beatings and '*was in fact in ignorance of what occurred in his camp*'. His second in command, Captain Komai Mitsuo, took full responsibility and was sentenced to death by hanging.

The court concluded that Major Chida, as camp commandant, was expected to be responsible for what went on in his camp. He may have been a puppet of Captain Komai, but that did not exonerate him. Major Chida was sentenced to eight years imprisonment. It is assumed this sentence and the previous one were served concurrently.

Major Chida was not accused of any crimes during his time as commander at Ubon. This is not to say that the regime at Ubon was any less easy, but evidence from Prisoners held there suggests that the Ubon camp was relatively trouble free.

The War Crimes Trial of Takamine

Takamine Iwayo was a Korean guard in the Imperial Japanese Army and was accused of war crimes that took place in Nong Pladuk, Bangkok and Ubon. His trial was held in Singapore on 2 and 3 August 1946. The charge sheet read:

Charge 1: Committing a war crime in that he at Nong Pladuk POW Camp, Siam, between 1 June 1944 and 31 December 1944, when as a member of staff of the said camp, in violation of the laws and usages of war, was concerned in the ill treatment of British POWs interned in the said camp, causing physical suffering to the said POWs and in particulate Sgt. C.W.J.Pratt and Pte. Barnet.

In the abstract of evidence of the trial, the extent of the brutality of which Takamine was capable was revealed. During a concert three performers were taken to the guard room and accused of insulting Japanese sergeants during their performance. Takamine kicked Sergeant Pratt in the legs and punched Private Kerswell and Lance Bombadier Owen. In the presence of Takamine, other Korean guards kicked Sergeant Pratt repeatedly in the stomach, which resulted in him being hospitalised for four weeks and being an outpatient for four months.

In addition, also at Nong Pladuk in the same period, Private Barnet was returning to the camp for a lunch break. He was so weak and debilitated from the effects of malaria that he could not walk or stand unsupported. Upon arriving in the camp, he collapsed in front of the guard room. Takamine beat Private Barnet repeatedly about the head and body with his feet and a bamboo stick until blood flowed freely. The other Prisoners supporting him were helpless and were told to move and leave Private Barnet where he lay without medical attention. He was still in the same condition when they returned after lunch and later that same evening at about 18:00 hours.

Private Barnet was eventually sent to Ubon. He was born on 30 April 1917 and lived in Brixton, London. He was a member of the East Surrey Regiment.

Charge 2: Committing a war crime in that he at Bangkok POW camp, Siam, at some day between 1 January 1945 and 31 March 1945, when as a member of the staff at the said camp, in violation of the laws and usages of war, did ill-treat Daniel Farnworth, a British POW interned in the said camp, causing physical suffering to the said POW Daniel Farnworth.

Private Farnworth was eventually sent to Ubon. He was born on 14 April 1918 and lived in Chorley, Lancashire. He was in the 18th Reconnaissance Corps.

Charge 3: Committing a war crime in that he at Ubon camp, Siam, between 1 March 1945 and 15 August 1945, when as a member of the staff of the said camp, in violation of the laws and usages of war, did ill-treat British POWs interned in the said camp causing physical suffering to the said POWs and in particular to Daniel Farnworth

In the abstract of evidence on this charge, it was stated that Takamine frequently beat Prisoners at Ubon. He struck Daniel Farnworth in the mouth with the butt of his rifle, knocking out two of Daniel's teeth and causing injury.

Takamine pleaded not guilty to each charge but he was found guilty and imprisoned for nine years.

The Sad Fate of Nai Thong In Phuriphat

Nai Thong In Phuriphat was the assemblyman (Member of Parliament) for Ubon and a government cabinet member when the Japanese entered Thailand. Prior to the arrival of the Japanese, he was openly critical of the government and some of its policies. In 1935 he filed a vote of no confidence in the State Council over several issues, including increased military collaboration with the government, an opium scandal, and an accusation of inefficiency by the Ministry of Economic Affairs. In 1937 he accused the government of allocating a disproportionate amount of funding to the military, comparing it to the lack of funding for education and public works. He then requested permission to set up a new political party, but the timing of the request was considered to be unsuitable and was rejected.

He was a close associate of Luang Pridi and most likely was present at the inaugural meeting of the Seri Thai Movement with his great friend, Nai Tiang Sirikhandra. In an interview in April 2016, with his daughter, Ora In Phuriphat, she described him as very wise man and smart with the family money. She said he had a photographic memory and was always working to improve his constituency with various schemes, particularly irrigation, which were vital to rice farming in the north east. Although he initially disagreed with the siting of Ubon's aerodrome, she affectionately called him a visionary.

Thongin became leader of Ubon's Seri Thai and secretly worked with an American trained OSS agent, Khun Karun Kengradomying, code name Ken, to set up a radio transmitter in the attic bedroom of the family home.

After the war, Thongin continued to serve Ubon as an assemblyman. In 1946 he helped to organise the left-wing Sahachip (Cooperative) party, whose nationalistic outlook was closely associated with neighbouring Indochina and Indonesia. The new party attracted the attention of the military and police. In 1947 both he and Nai Tiang Sirikhandra were arrested and charged with *'conspiring to subordinate Thai national identity within a larger communist-dominated South East Asia union'*. The military fabricated stories of communist plots, in which they accused Thongin of concealing Russian weapons at his house in Ubon that were intended for a revolution. The case was dismissed but the suspicion remained.

By the end of 1948, the activities of Thongin and his associates were subjected to increased scrutiny. He was arrested again, together with his brother Nai Thim Phuriphat, Nai Tiang Sirikhandra, Chamlong Daorueang (from Mahasarakham), Thongplaeo Chonlaphum (from Nakhon Nayok) and Thawin Udon (from Roi Et). They were charged with planning to separate the north-east area from the rest of Thailand and join up the area with Indochina in a communist-dominated South East Asian Union. They were released but in March 1949 Thongin, Chamlong, Thongplaeo and Thawin were re-arrested following the discovery of Luang Pridi's plot to overthrow Luang Phibul who, by now, had been reinstated as prime minister.

The four men were tortured, resulting in broken legs, cigar burns and bruises to the face. Following their beating, the accused were transferred by bus from one prison to another. On the journey the bus suddenly stopped. Gunfire followed and the four Prisoners were shot and killed. The encounter became known as the 'Kilo 11 Incident'. The official police account stated that the bus was ambushed by sympathisers of the accused in an attempt to rescue them. A gunfight ensued, and all four Prisoners were killed. However, it was recorded that neither the driver of the bus nor any of the police guarding the men were injured or killed in any crossfire. Nai Tiang Sirikhandra was killed in a separate incident (details not known) in 1952.

The death of Thongin and his associates had a profound effect on the north-east region. It was apparent that they were killed because they supported Luang Pridi, whose effectiveness in government had significantly receded in the post-war years, and because they had been singled out as troublemakers. Their deaths drew attention to the indifference of central government towards the north-east region and created the foundations for a new political identity for the north east.

Sadly, following this tragic incident those who had supported the Seri Thai against the Japanese were fearful that their previous association might be used against them. Subsequently they rarely spoke of their experiences and even fewer wrote down their stories.

EPILOGUE

The land on which the camp was built is now divided into small rice fields and pasture for cattle. However, there are small sections where it is possible to see vague remnants of camp features such as a small section of the deep moat that surrounded the camp. This is very overgrown and relatively short in length, but it is plainly not a natural feature and, although no plan of the camp has so far been discovered, local anecdotal evidence suggests it is part of the original moat.

Close by the moat is the site of the kitchen. The bricks used to make the oven were removed by famers to make their rice fields but they were re-discovered in a bund created to retain water in the field. Local farmers have found Japanese coins but nothing else has been so far discovered except a Japanese bomb casing and bomb fragments. Water is still drawn from underground wells, although plastic pipes have replaced bamboo ones.

The airstrip is located about one mile west of the camp. Today only the southern section of the original airstrip remains, which is six hundred metres long. A concrete runway was added about twenty years ago, but this is only about five metres wide. The original width of the airstrip is clearly visible although it is covered in bushes and scrubland.

This section is used by several people, including an amateur pilot who flies a two-seater light aircraft that is kept in a modern hangar at the edge of the airstrip. Other users are amateur model-aeroplane enthusiasts and occasional motor-powered paragliders. Cows graze on the sparse grass, and part of it is used as an access route for surrounding villages. On this section there is evidence of the three craters where Japanese ordnance was destroyed. Bomb fragments have been discovered along the full length of this section.

The northern half of the airstrip has been left to nature; it is fenced off and impenetrable. The land is now owned by the Royal Thai Army, but the Royal Thai Air Force maintain an operational radio station at the far northern end of the original airstrip.

Adjacent to the radio station is the section of road built by the Prisoners to link the airstrip construction site to the main road, which is now Highway 212. Today this road forms a side road that runs due west to access local villages.

About one-and-a-half miles due south of the airstrip lies the location where Major Smiley put down the Japanese horses. This area was identified by Khun Thongdee Wongman in 2016 and verified by local residents, but the fields are now dense with trees and bushes and there is no sign of the remains.

There are few physical remains to remind us about the year in which Ubon was dominated by the Japanese and the Prisoner of War camp.

Visitors to Ubon fly into the airport not knowing that they have arrived at a place where there is a slice of interesting World War Two history. If they go to Thung Si Muang park in the centre of Ubon they will see the Monument of Merit memorial and possibly come away wanting to know more about what it represents. There is a lot of history embedded in its foundations which this story has sought to bring to light.

It is a fascinating insight of the Prisoner's daily life in the camp and its unique liberation. But behind that story is a surprising chain of events involving the SOE the Seri Thai with an interesting mix of international and national politics and politicians and military rivalries.

But most importantly it is a story of human courage and freedom: the courage of the Prisoners to survive their ordeal; the courage of the Seri Thai resistance and its leaders to face up to the Japanese; the courage of the British SOE liberators, who operated behind the Japanese lines at great risk to their lives; the courage of Thailand's eminent politicians, who would not accept the presence of the Japanese and had the tenacity to contact the Allies and the faith that they would respond. And, not least, the courage, compassion and collective 'good heart' of the Ubon people who looked after the men before they left for home.

Freedom was secured for everyone when the Japanese surrendered in August 1945 after Hiroshima and Nagasaki.

LEST WE FORGET

APPENDIX: Analysis of Ubon Medical Diary

The list below identifies the ex-POWs with dysentery when Ubon camp was liberated in August 1945. These men were repatriated before any other ex-POWs. The different discharge dates probably indicate the severity of their condition.

Record admitted	Name Date discharge	Reg No Condition	Unit	Date
17555	Pte Freestone 10/09/45	4858348 Amoebic dysentery	Leics	26/05/45
17719	Gnr Tate 19/09/45	1629299 Chronic diarrhoea	5S/L	03/08/45
17735	Sig Hughes 23/09/45	2368805 Bacillary dysentery	RCS	06/08/45
17768	Fus Allen 18/09/45	4278352 Bacillary dysentery	RNF	12/08/45
17764	Bdr Shepard 15/09/45	909511 Amoebic dysentery	118FR	12/08/45
17777	Sgt Gripton 04/09/45	922750 Amoebic dysentery	135FR	15/08/45
17778	Pte Turner 16/09/45	3859164 Bacillary dysentery	RECCE	15/08/45
17792	Dvr Phillips 23/09/45	2585741 Bacillary dysentery	RCS	18/08/45
17798	L/C Rogers 03/09/45	2185699 Bacillary dysentery	RE	19/08/45
17807	Fus Selkeld 04/09/45	4275458 Bacillary dysentery	RNF	20/08/45

17819	Pte Bullock 16/09/45	4976831 Sher F Bacillary dysentery	24/08/45
17825	Pdr Smith 08/09/45	58377723 135FR Bacillary dysentery	26/08/45
17831	Pte Richards 10/09/45	7368933 RAMC Bacillary dysentery	27/08/45
17846	Pte Burstow 09/09/45	6918659 RECCE Bacillary dysentery	30/08/45
17847	Sig Dolan 11/09/45	2335120 RCS Bacillary dysentery	30/08/45
17849	Pte Green 10/09/45	NZ50060 AIF Bacillary dysentery	31/08/45
17850	Stickley 11/09/45	T/13036269 RASC Bacillary dysentery	31/08/45

The list below shows a general analysis of the various medical conditions reported in the Ubon Medical Diary

Cases	Diagnosis Number of POWs	Number of
Beriberi	7	7
Blackwater fever	7	7
Bronchitis related	23	18
Cellulitis	5	5
Cystitis	11	8
Diarrhoea	48	46
Dysentery	122	110
Enteritis	6	6
Gastritis	7	7
Hepatitis related	9	8
IAT	23	22
Injury	14	14
Jaundice	27	26
Malaria	194	169
Other	98	92
Pellegra	18	17
Peptic ulcer	9	9
Renal cholic	16	14
Tachycardia	13	11
Ulcers and abscesses	49	46
TOTAL	706	642*

*Total of POWs (642) includes POWs admitted more than once for the same condition or different conditions (there were approximately 536 individual POWs admitted).

INDEX

A

B

D

E

F

G

H

I

J

K

L

M

222

North Texas State University, 60

O

P

229

T

U

Warrant Officer II Charles Steel, 50, 63, 65, 66, 79, 80, 82, 83, 114, 144, 152
Warrant Officer S.J. Slotboom, 61, 151
Udon Thani, 94, 99, 118, 131, 132, 143, 193
Ulcers, 212
UNESCO, 52
United States
    131st Field Artillery, 102, 105
    Air Force, 96, 105
    Japan declaration of war, 26
    Navy, 101
    OSS, 122
    OSS support Luang Pridi, 115
    OSS trained Thai agents, 110
    Relations with Thailand, 16, 19, 22, 23
    Seri Thai, 15, 30, 34, 35, 36, 108
    Thailand declaration of war, 14, 23, 32, 33, 35, 42
    War with Japan, 25, 34
    West Point, 193
    XO Group, 32
USS Houston, 101, 102
USS Missouri, 147

V

V Scheme, 149
VE Day, 160
Vichy French, 18, 19, 43
Vientiane, 137, 182
Viet Minh, 198
Vietnam, 21, 177
Vietnam war, 96, 184, 199

W

Wampo Viaduct, 105
Warin Chamrap, 55, 93, 94, 140, 142, 150, 165, 172, 186, 191, 197
Washington D.C., 33, 35, 112, 183
Wing Commander Hodges, 125
Wing-Commander Manop Souriya, 193
Winston Churchill, 116

X

XO Group, 31, 32

Y

Bibliography

Books

Banomyong, P. (2000) *Pridi by Pridi*. Chiang Mai, Silkworm Books.

Banomyong, P. (1979?) *Political and Military Tasks of the Free-Thai Movement to Regain National Sovereignty and Independence*. Thailand, Publisher not identified.

Barber, N. (1968) *Sinister Twilight*. London, Collins.

Beattie, R. (2015) *The Death Railway*. Kanchanaburi, T.B.R.C. Co Ltd.

Churchill, H. (2005) *Prisoners on the Kwai*. Dereham, Larks Press.

Crager, K.E. (2008) *Hell Under the Rising Sun*. Texas, A&M University Press.

Crosby, Sir J. (1945) *Siam: The Crossroads*. London, Hollis & Carter.

Cruickshank, Dr C. (1983) *SOE in the Far East*. Oxford, Oxford University Press.

Davies, P.N. (1991) *The Man Behind the Bridge*. London, The Athlone Press Ltd.

Dewey, J & S. (2014) *PoW Sketchbook – a story of survival*. Wallingford, Pie Powder Press.

Eldredge, S.A. (2014) *Captive Audiences/Captive Performers*. Digital Commons Macalester College online.

Fyans, P. (2011) *Captivity, Slavery and Survival as a Far East POW*. Barnsley, Pen & Sword Books Ltd.

Gideonse, H. (1989) *Het Vergeten Leger In De Jungle*. Amsterdam, De Bataafsche Leeuw.

Gilchrist, Sir A. (1970) *Bangkok Top Secret*. London, Hutchison & Co.

Haseman, J.B. (2002) *The Thai Resistance Movement During World War II*. Chiang Mai, Silkworm Books.

Hedley, J. (1996) *Jungle Fighter*. Brighton, Tom Donovan Publishing Ltd.

Jayanama, D. (1966) *Siam and World War II*. Bangkok, The Social Science Association of Thailand Press.

Jones, C. (2019) *The Clandestine Lives of Colonel David Smiley*. Edinburgh, Edinburgh University Press Ltd.

Kemp, P. (1961) *Alms for Oblivion*. London, Cassell & Company Ltd.

Keyes, C. (2013) *Finding Their Voice: Northeastern Villagers and the Thai State*. Chaing Mai, Silkworm Books

Kratoska, P.H. (2006) *The Thailand-Burma Railway, 1942-1946: War Crimes*. London, Taylor & Francis Ltd.

Kratoska, P.H. (2005) *The Thailand-Burma Railway 1942-1946: Documents and Selected Writings*. London, Taylor & Francis Ltd.

McDonald, E. (1993) *Undercover Girl*. Time Life Books

O'Brien, T. (1987) *The Moonlight War*. London, William Collins & Sons Co. Ltd.

Reynolds, E.B. (2004) *Thailand's Secret War*. Cambridge, Cambridge University Press.

Sresik, Dr S. (not known) Seri Thai in north-east Thailand. (translated from Thai).

Smiley, D. (1994) *Irregular Regular*. Norwich, Michael Russell (Publishing) Ltd.

Smith, N. & Clark, B. (1946) *Into Siam, Underground Kingdom*. New York, Bobbs-Merrill Company.

Spencer-Chapman, F. (1949) *The Jungle is Neutral*. London, Chatto and Windus.

Steel, C. & Best, B. (2004) *Secret Letters from the Railway*. Barnsley, Pen & Sword Books Ltd.

Summers, J. (2006) *The Colonel of Tarmakan*. London, Pocket Books.

Sweet-Escott, B. (1965) *Baker Street Irregular*. London, Methuen & Co Ltd.

Tsuji, Masanobu. (1960) *Singapore the Japanese Version*. Sydney, Ure Smith Pty Ltd.

Weygers, L.J. (1999) *A Dutch POW in Thailand. (Four Years Till Tomorrow edited by Tromp, S.G.)*. Surrey (British Columbia, Canada), Vanderheide Publishing Co. Ltd.

Wiriyawit, W. (1997) Free Thai. Bangkok, White Lotus Co.Ltd.

Young, E.M. (1995) *Aerial Nationalism*. Washington & London, Smithsonian Institution Press.

Primary Sources

Australia
Australian Government Defence Honours and Awards Appeal Tribunal report 7 September 2017
Private Records Collection Australian War Memorial Hugh King Ashby: PR03218

Imperial War Museum London
IWM catalogue 23188, 22 May 2002 Captain Eric Martin (Oral History).
IWM Photographs Service of Colonel David Smiley with Force 136 (SOE) in Thailand March – December 1945.
IWM Catalogue 10340 (1988) Smiley, David De Crespigny (Oral History).

Public Records National Archives Kew
Special Operations Executive: Series HS1 53; HS1 55; HS1 57; HS1 58; HS1 60; HS1 63; HS1 67; HS1 68; HS1 77; HS1 88; HS1 326; HS7 188; HS1 307; HS1 326.
War Office: Series WO 208/1920; WO 208/1877; WO 347/4; WO 361/1120.
Op Rep 297

United States
Marcello, R. E. (1977) *Thomas Whitehead interview with North Texas State University.* North Texas State University Oral History Collection 366
United States National Archives and Records Administration. OSS Current Intelligence Study No 4, 30 March 1944
United States National Archives and Records Administration. OSS Intelligence Reports May 1945

Other Public Records
Arian Roos Gerritje report Dutch National Archive Transfer of Dutch to Bali and Lombok
R & A report 1007, dated 15 May 1944
RAPWI Sit Reps 2, 28 August, 3 29 August and 4 30 August 1945

RAPWI Sit Rep 16, 10 September 1945
Force 136 Sit Rep 20, September 1945
SACSEA report to Cabinet Office, 5 October 1945
SACSEA WIS No 102, 31 October 1945
SEAC Ops report, 25 October 1945
SEAC Ops report, 26 October 1945
SEAC Ops report, 19 November 1945
Thailand: Train Schedules and Shipments to and from Bangkok, dated 4 July 1946.

Personal Interviews
Ban Nong Tokaew (Ubon) Village elders, 5 December 2018
Khun Gim Jiarajinda, (Ubon) May 2015 and March 2019
Khun Preecha Petin, (Ubon) December 2018
Khun Ora In Phuriphat, (Ubon) 11 April 2016
Khun Thongdee Wongman, (Ubon) August 2018
Tom Brown, (Gosport) June 2018 and September 2018
Harold Pleasance (Stratford) September 2016

Articles
Neves, M.S.P., Barata, J.M.M. & Silva, A.R.R. (2016) *The First Aerial Journey from Portugal to Macau.* Online at researchgate.net
Wexler, R.L. (1970) *A Comparison of Annual Rainfall Probabilities in Thailand and the Canal Zone Vicinity.* Massachusetts, U.S. army Natick Laboratories.
Snelling, S. (2013) *Far East Escape.* Online at www.docdroid.net
Whincup, E.W. (date unknown) *Speedo Speedo The beginning and End of an Epic in the Life of a Japanese POW.* Personal account unpublished.

Newspapers
Chelmsford Chronicle 21 September 1945
Derby Evening Telegraph 14 September 1945
Evening Despatch 11 January 1941
Kalgoorlie Miner 19 February 1947
Lancashire Daily Post 22 September 1945
New York Times
Queensland Times 9 January 1941
Sevenoaks Chronicle and Kentish Advertiser 28 September 1945

Sydney Morning Herald 16 December 1940
Townsville Daily Bulletin Friday 9 November 1945
Western Australian 17, 18, 22 January 1941
Western Gazette 21 September 1945
Worthing Gazette 28 November 1945

Websites
www.stonebooks.com/history/vichyvssiam.shtml, Stone, B. (1988)
Indochina Siam conflict 1940-41
www.japansekrijgsgevangenkampen.nl/Ubon.htm. Dutch POW
Ubon
www.roycollins.me.uk Roy Collins Memorial
Quirk, R. www.rquirk.com SEAC RAF consolidated Liberator
Squadrons
www.creopcrown.co.uk Operation Crown
www.mansell.com Letter from Preston L. Clark to Captain
Norwood, 20 May 1946
www.legal-tools.org/en/doc/e3a78d/ Major Chida War crimes
www.legal-tools.org/doc/823008/pdf/ Takamine War crime trial
www.gahetna.nl Dutch military archive

Other Sources
Maurice Naylor: VJ Day speech at St Martins in the Field, 15
August 2012 courtesy of M. Naylor
M. Soesman: notes (provided by Henk Beekhuis)
Extract from Colonel Toosey's final report courtesy of Julie
Summers
Newsphere Ubon camp newsletter editions 1, 2, 3 reproduced with
kind permission of Fenella France
Personal documents of Thomas Whitehead courtesy of Timothy
Whitehead.
Personal documents of Len Knott courtesy of Kathy Knott.
Personal documents of John Sartin courtesy of David Sartin
Drawings produced by William Wilder courtesy of Anthony Wilder
Drawings produced by Donovan 'Nobby' Clarke courtesy of Greta
Palmer and Michael Clarke

Gallery

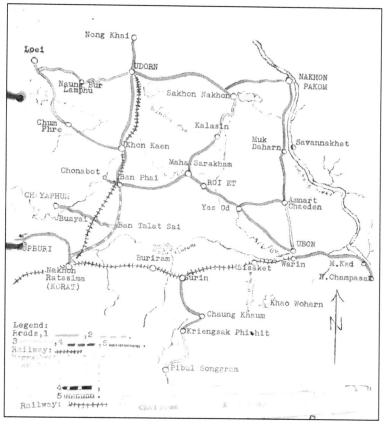

North-east Thailand – Operation Candle
(Courtesy of National Archives Kew)

Drawing of Ubon
camp by William
Wilder
(Drawing © Anthony Wilder)

Drawing of Ubon
camp theatre by
Donovan Clarke
(Drawing © Greta Palmer and
Mike Clarke)

Drawing of Ubon
camp kitchen by
Donovan Clarke
(Drawing © Greta Palmer and
Mike Clarke)

Major David Smiley
(Courtesy of Major David Smiley's family and *Daily Telegraph*)

Major John Hedley
(Courtesy of Tom Donovan of Tom Donovan Publishing)

Colonel Phillip Toosey
(Courtesy of Toosey family)

Major Peter Kemp
(Courtesy of Christopher Othen)

Major Chita Sotomatsu
(Courtesy of Rod Beatty Thailand–Burma Railway Centre, Kanchanaburi, Thailand)

Private Robert Merritt
(Courtesy of 2/2nd Pioneer Battalion)

Ubon camp's *Newsphere* newsletter Issues 1, 2 and 3
Ubon camp airstrip in 2019
(*Newsphere* reproduced with kind permission of Fenella France ©Fenella France.
Airstrip photo ©Ray Withnall collection)

Drawing of Supply Drop by Liberator aircraft
at Ubon camp by Donovan Clarke
(Drawing © Greta Palmer and Mike Clarke reproduced with their kind permission)

Monument of Merit in December 1945
(Photo © Smiley family. Reproduced with their kind permission. Image provided by Imperial War Museum London)

Monument of Merit in the 1960s
(Reproduced with permission from *A History of Ubon* by Chooniyom)

Monument of Merit 2019
(©Ray Withnall collection)

Site of the former Ubon camp and aerial view of airstrip 2019
(©Ray Withnall collection)

Recovered bricks hand made by the Ubon Prisoners
for their kitchen oven
(©Ray Withnall collection)

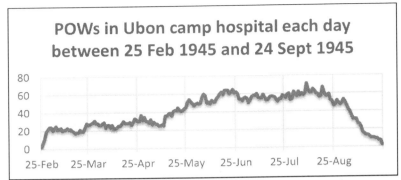

The number of POWs in the hospital on any given day
(©Ray Withnall collection)

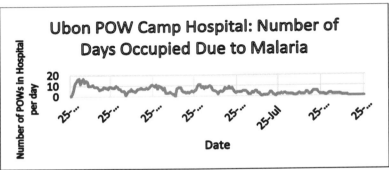

Weekly admissions due to malaria
(©Ray Withnall collection)

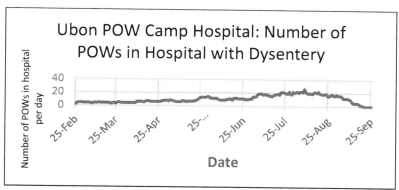

Weekly admissions due to dysentery
(©Ray Withnall collection)